A-Z BASINGSTOKE

CONT[ENTS]

Key to Map Pages	2-3
Map Pages	4-39

[...0-52]

REFER[ENCE]

Motorway	**M3**	Car Park (selected)		**P**
A Road	A30	Church or Chapel		†
B Road	B3400	Fire Station		■
Dual Carriageway		Hospital		**H**
One-way Street		House Numbers (A & B Roads only)		57 44
Traffic flow on A roads is also indicated by a heavy line on the driver's left.		Information Centre		🅸
Under Construction Road		National Grid Reference		⁴55
Opening dates are correct at the time of publication.		Park & Ride		Leisure Park **P+R**
Proposed Road		Police Station		▲
Restricted Access		Post Office		★
Pedestrianized Road		Safety Camera with Speed Limit		**30**
Track / Footpath		Fixed cameras and long term road work cameras. Symbols do not indicate camera direction.		
Residential Walkway		Toilet:		
Railway	Station / Tunnel / Level Crossing	without facilities for the Disabled		▽
		with facilities for the Disabled		▽
Built-up Area	DUKE ST	Educational Establishment		▨
Local Authority Boundary	— · — · —	Hospital or Healthcare Building		▨
Posttown Boundary	————	Industrial Building		▨
Postcode Boundary (within Posttown)	— — — —	Leisure or Recreational Facility		▨
		Place of Interest		▨
		Public Building		▨
		Shopping Centre or Market		▨
Map Continuation	▲ 20	Other Selected Buildings		▨

SCALE

1:19,000

0 ¼ ½ Mile

0 250 500 750 Metres 1 Kilometre

3 ⅓ inches (8.47 cm) to 1 mile
5.26 cm to 1km

Copyright of Geographers' A-Z Map Company Limited

Fairfield Road, Borough Green, Sevenoaks, Kent TN15 8PP
Telephone: 01732 781000 (Enquiries & Trade Sales)
01732 783422 (Retail Sales)
www.az.co.uk
Copyright © Geographers' A-Z Map Co. Ltd.
Edition 3 2013

 **Ordnance Survey®** This product includes mapping data licensed from Ordnance Survey® with the permission of the Controller of Her Majesty's Stationery Office.

© Crown Copyright 2012. All rights reserved. Licence number 100017302
Safety camera information supplied by www.PocketGPSWorld.com
Speed Camera Location Database Copyright 2012 © PocketGPSWorld.com

G000109744

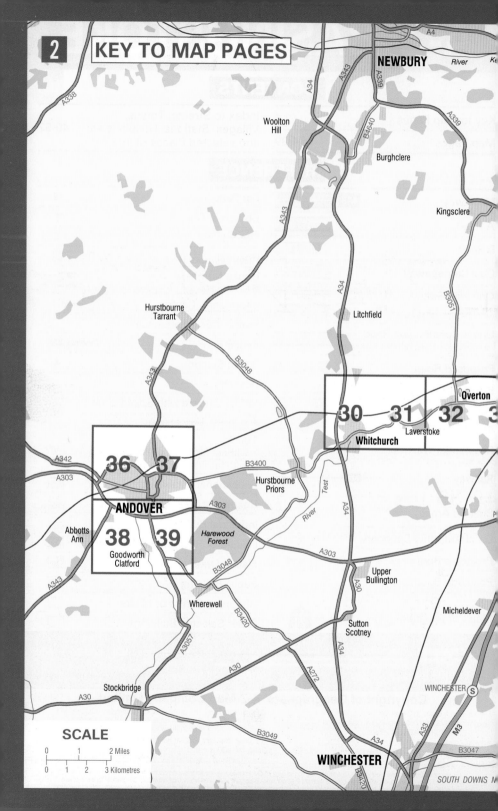

KEY TO MAP PAGES

A4

NEWBURY River Ke

A338

A34

A343

A339

Woolton
Hill

B4640

Burghclere

A339

Kingsclere

A34

B3051

Hurstbourne
Tarrant

Litchfield

A343

B3048

Overton

30 31 32 3

Laverstoke

Whitchurch

A342

36 37

B3400

A303

Hurstbourne
Priors

Test

A34

River

ANDOVER

A303

Abbotts
Ann

38 39

Harewood
Forest

A303

A34

A343

Goodworth
Clatford

B3048

Upper
Bullington

A30

Wherewell

B3420

Micheldever

A3057

Sutton
Scotney

A34

A30

A272

WINCHESTER (S)

Stockbridge

A30

A33

M3

B3049

A34

B3047

WINCHESTER

B3420

SOUTH DOWNS N

SCALE

0   1   2 Miles

0   1   2   3 Kilometres

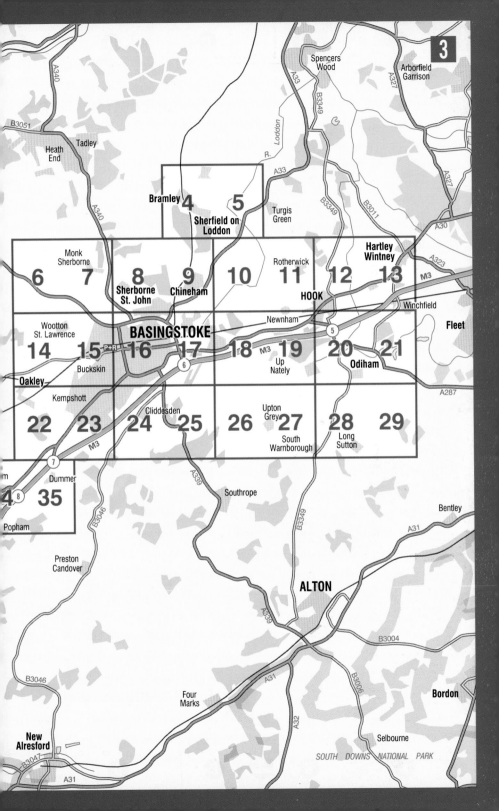

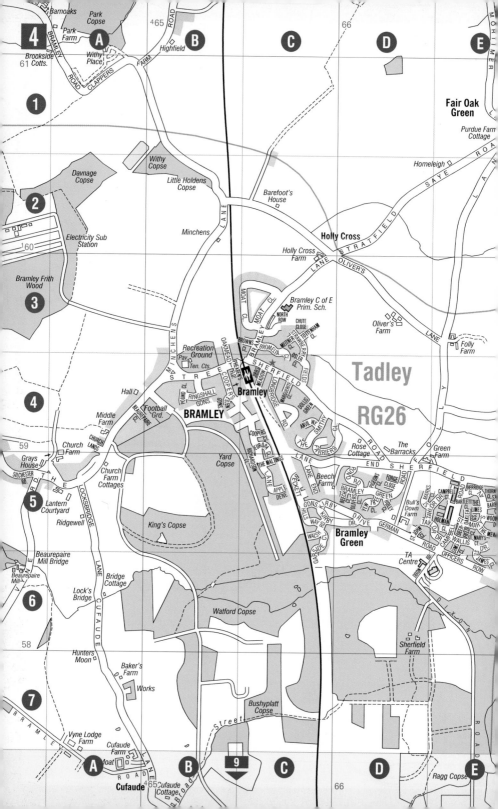

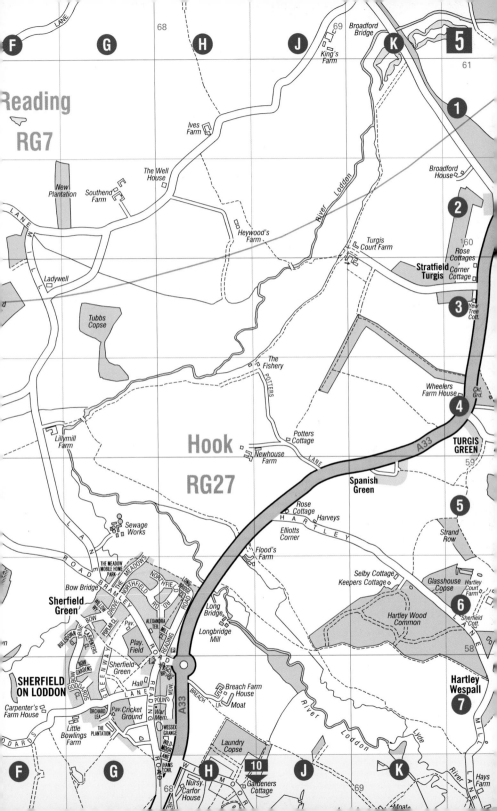

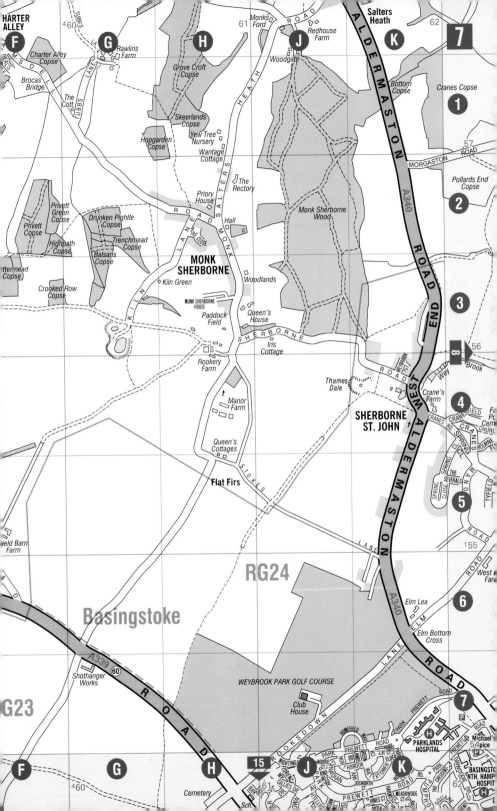

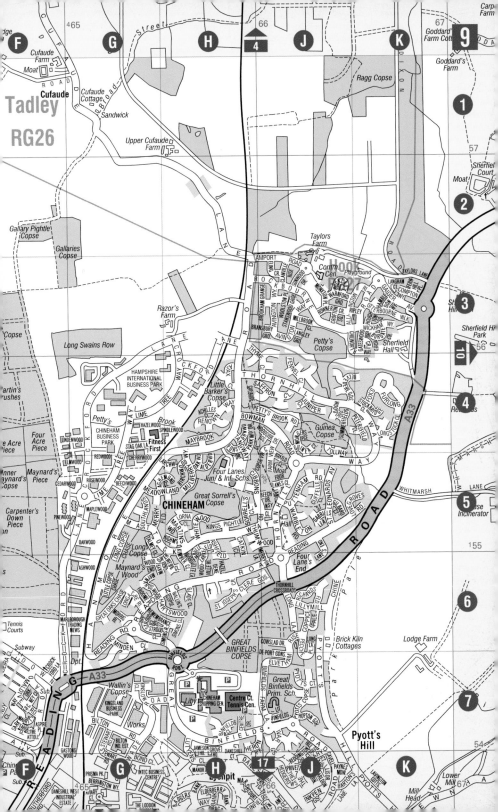

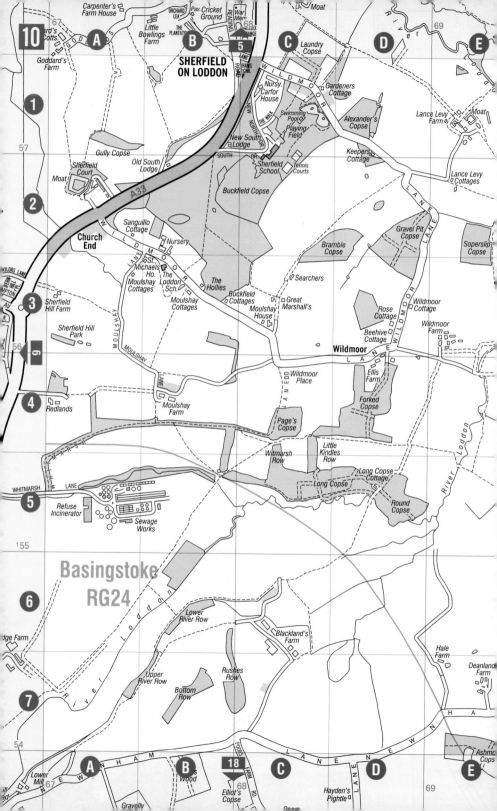

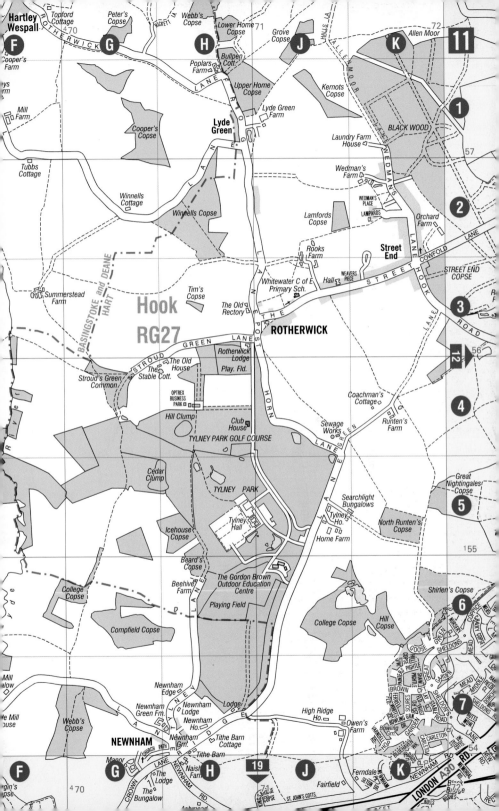

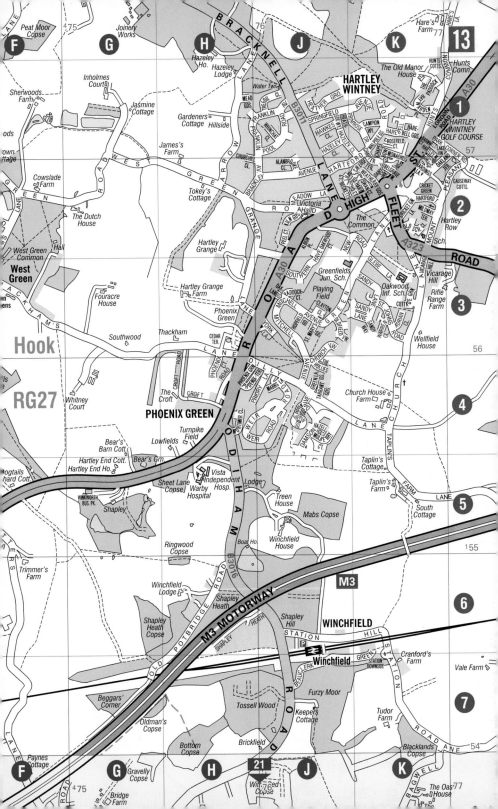

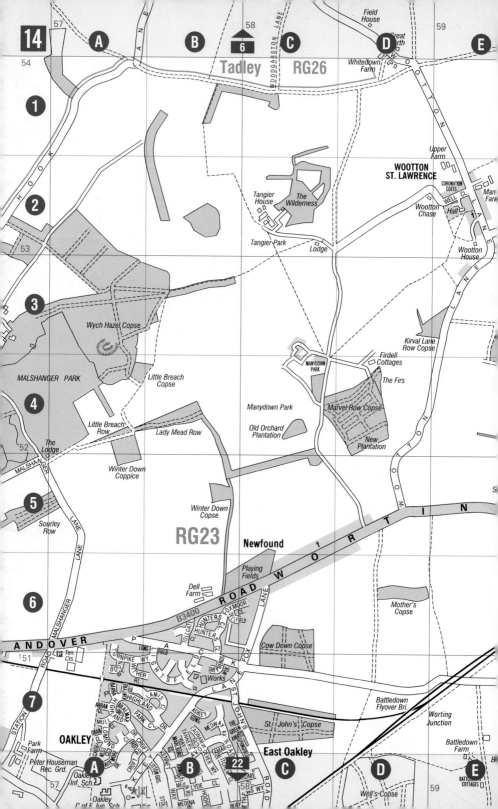

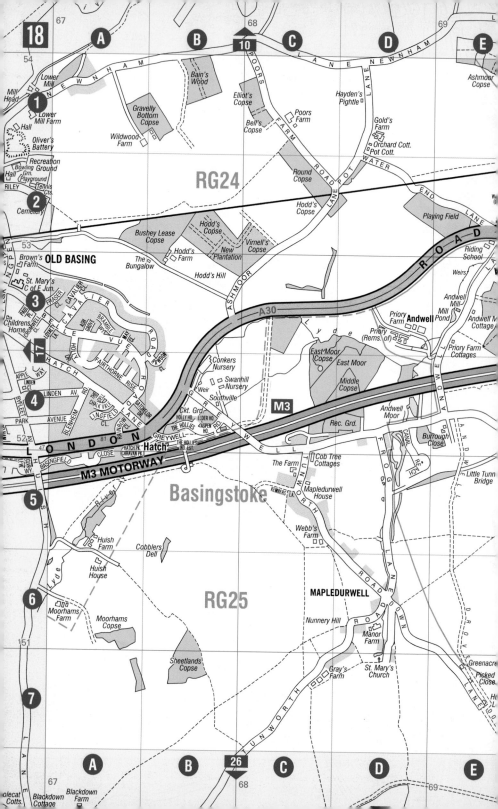

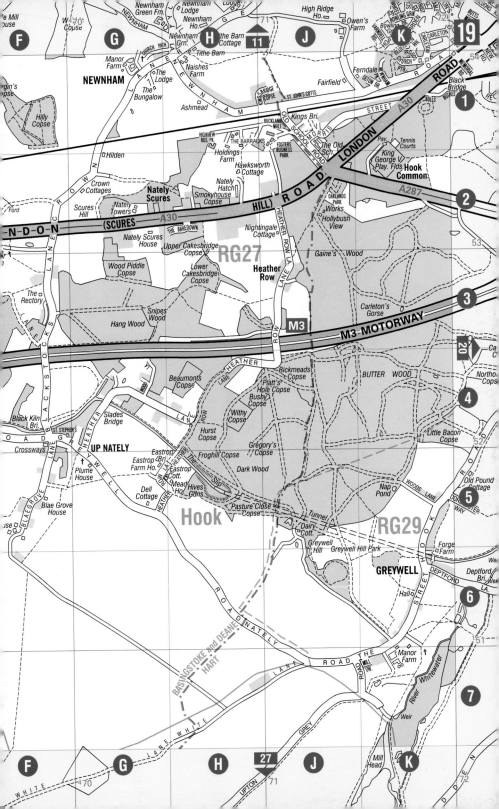

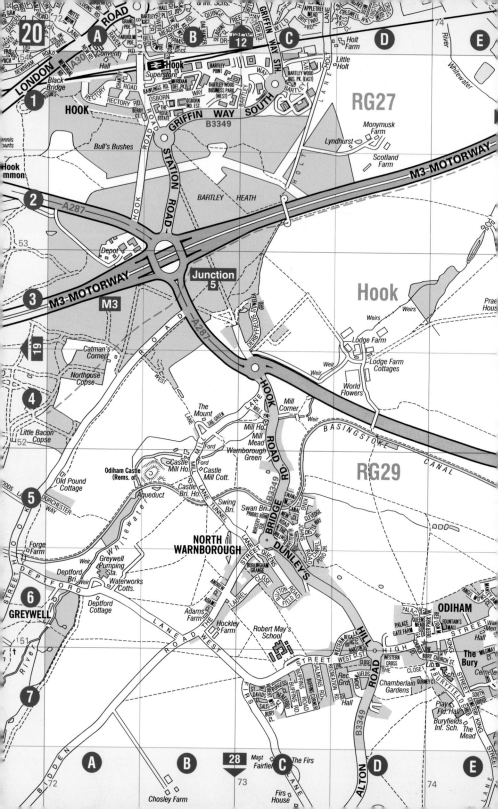

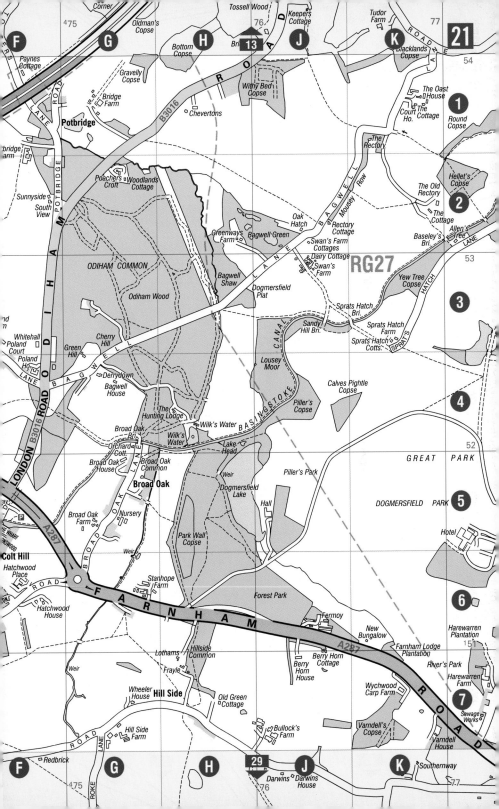

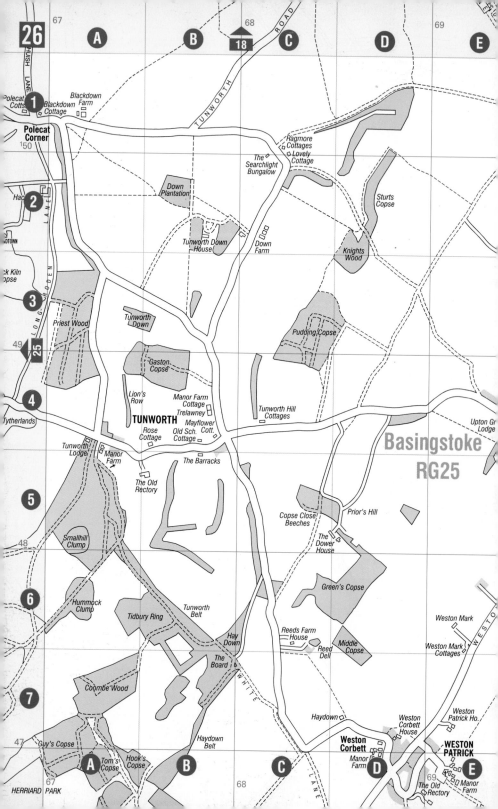

67 68 69

A B C D E

18

BUSH LANE
TUNWORTH ROAD

Polecat Cotts
Blackdown Cottage
Blackdown Farm

Polecat Corner
150

Hac
2

LANE
DTOWN

k Kiln
opse

3

LONG LODEN

49
25

4

Tytherlands

TUNWORTH

Ragmore Cottages
Lovely Cottage

The Searchlight Bungalow

Down Plantation

Tunworth Down House

Down Farm

Sturts Copse

Knights Wood

Priest Wood

Tunworth Down

Gaston Copse

Lion's Row

Rose Cottage

Manor Farm Cottage
Trelawney
Mayflower Cott.
Old Sch. Cottage

Pudding Copse

Tunworth Hill Cottages

Basingstoke RG25

Upton Gr Lodge

Tunworth Lodge
Manor Farm

The Barracks

The Old Rectory

5

48

Smallhill Clump

Copse Close Beeches
Prior's Hill

The Dower House

6

Hummock Clump

Tidbury Ring

Tunworth Belt

Green's Copse

Weston Mark

Weston Mark Cottages

WESTO

Hay Down

Reeds Farm House

Reed Dell

Middle Copse

7

Coombe Wood

The Board

WHITE

Haydown

Weston Corbett House

Weston Patrick Ho.

47

Guy's Copse

Tom's Copse
Hook's Copse

Haydown Belt

Weston Corbett
Manor Farm

WESTON PATRICK

The Old Rectory
Manor Farm

A B C D E

HERRIARD PARK

67 68 69

LANE

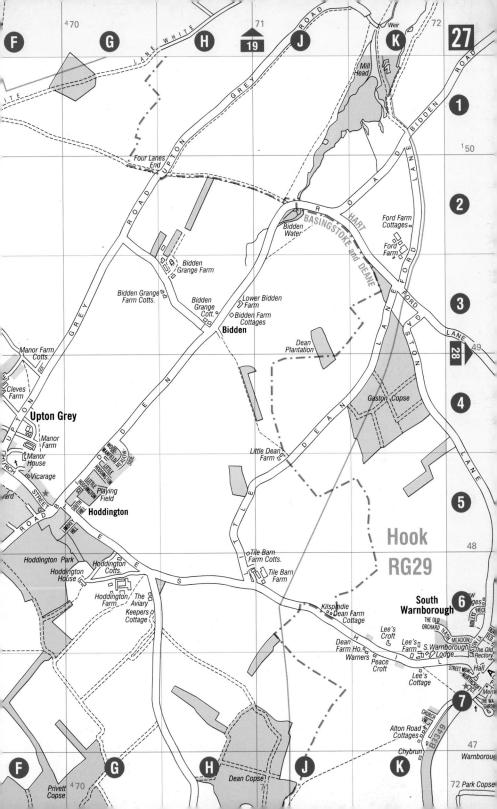

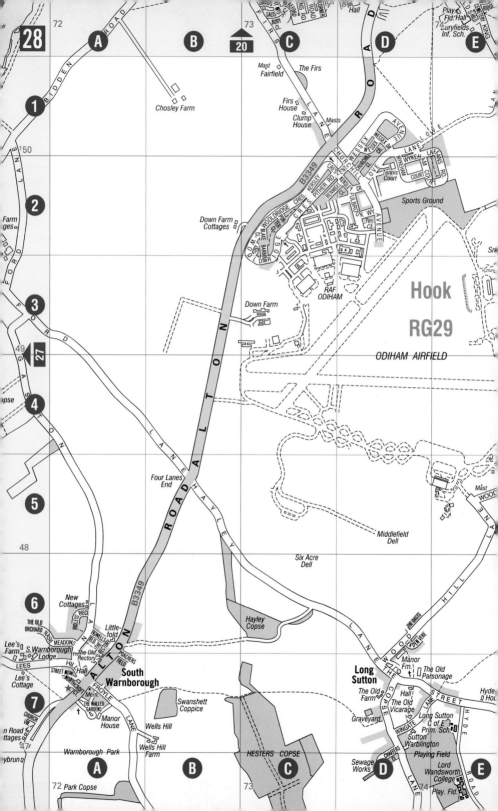

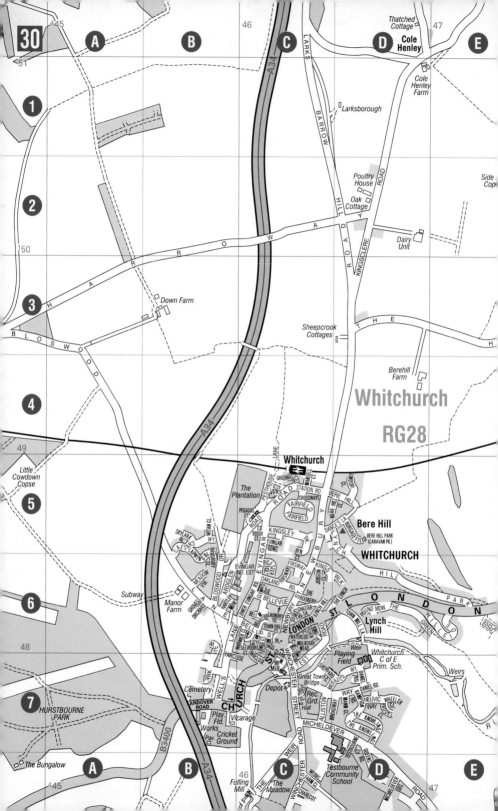

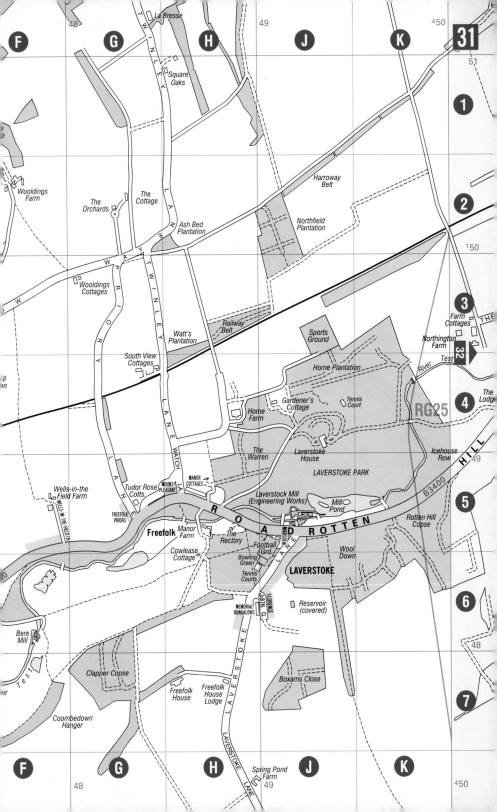

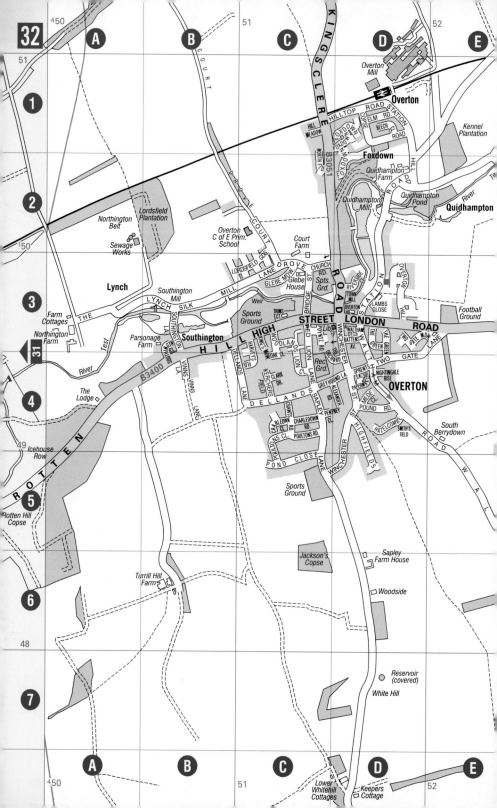

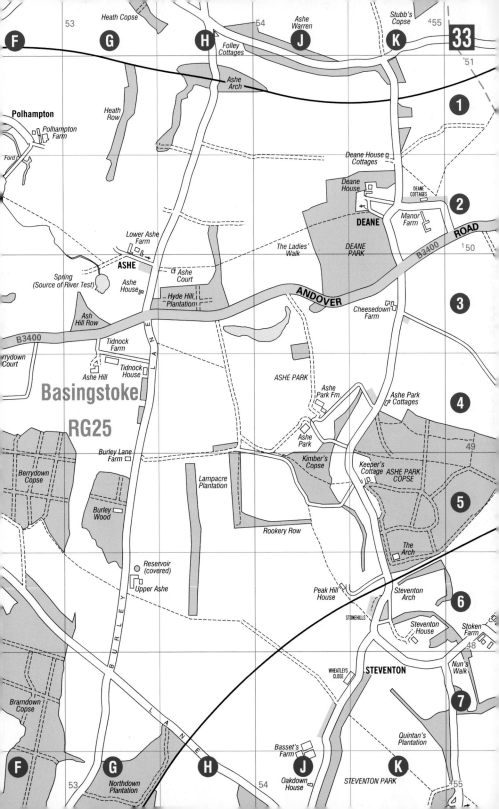

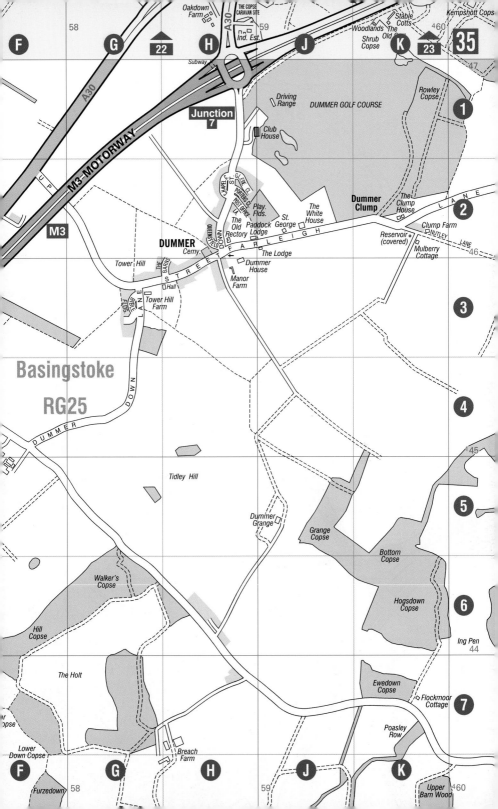

F   58   **G**   **22**   **H**   59   **J**   **K**   **23**   **35**

Oakdown Farm

THE COPSE CARAVAN SITE

A30

Ind. Est.

Subway

Woodlands Copse
Shrub Copse
Stable Cotts
The Old

Kempshott Cops

460

47

Driving Range

DUMMER GOLF COURSE

Rowley Copse

1

Club House

Junction 7

M3-MOTORWAY

UP

M3

GLEBE CL.
PORTERS CL.
CHAPEL LA.
POST OFFICE
Play. Flds.
St. George
The White House
Dummer Clump
The Clump House

LANE

2

QUEENFIELD
The Old Rectory
Paddock Lodge

Clump Farm
NUTLEY
LANE
46

DUMMER
Cerny.

Reservoir (covered)

Mulberry Cottage

Tower Hill

THE BARN

The Lodge

Dummer House

FARLEIGH

3

STREET

Manor Farm

Hall

Tower Hill Farm

DOWN LANE
STABLE

Basingstoke

RG25

DUMMER
DOWN
LANE

4

145

Tidley Hill

Dummer Grange

5

Grange Copse

Bottom Copse

Walker's Copse

Hogsdown Copse

6

Hill Copse

Ing Pen
44

The Holt

Ewedown Copse

Flockmoor Cottage

7

Poasley Row

Lower Down Copse

Breach Farm

Upper Barn Wood

Furzedown

F   58   **G**   **H**   59   **J**   **K**   460

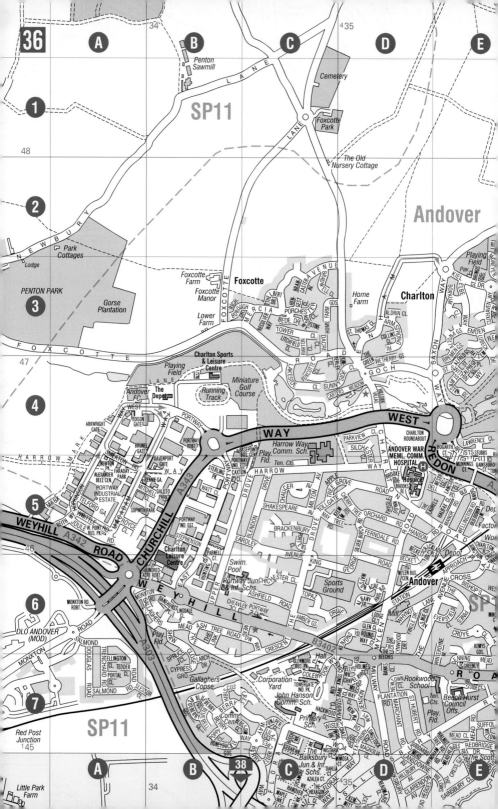

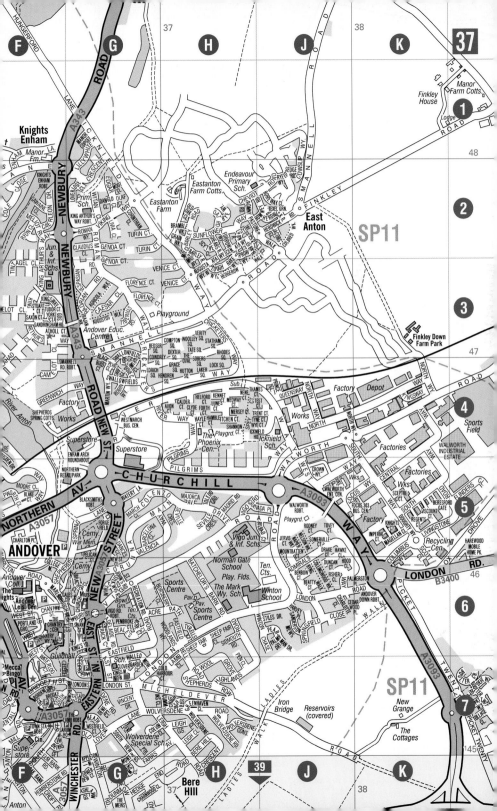

INDEX

Including Streets, Places & Areas, Hospitals etc., Industrial Estates,
Selected Flats & Walkways, Stations and Selected Places of Interest.

HOW TO USE THIS INDEX

1. Each street name is followed by its Postcode District, then by its Locality abbreviation(s) and then by its map reference;
   e.g. **Abbey Rd.** RG24: B'toke . . . .1B **16** is in the RG24 Postcode District and the Basingstoke Locality and is to be found in square 1B on page **16**.
   The page number is shown in bold type.

2. A strict alphabetical order is followed in which Av., Rd., St., etc. (though abbreviated) are read in full and as part of the street name;
   e.g. **Apple Tree Gro.** appears after **Appletree Cl.** but before **Appletree Mead**

3. Streets and a selection of flats and walkways that cannot be shown on the mapping, appear in the index with the thoroughfare to which
   they are connected shown in brackets; e.g. **Alders Cl.** RG21: B'toke . . . .4F **17** (off The Moorings)

4. Addresses that are in more than one part are referred to as not continuous.

5. Places and areas are shown in the index in BLUE TYPE and the map reference is to the actual map square in which the town centre or area is located
   and not to the place name shown on the map; e.g. ANDOVER 7F 37

6. An example of a selected place of interest is Andover Mus. 6G 37

7. An example of a station is Andover Station (Rail) . . . .6E 36, also included is Park & Ride.
   e.g. Leisure Park (Park & Ride) 4K 15

8. An example of a Hospital, Hospice or selected Healthcare facility is ANDOVER WAR MEMORIAL COMMUNITY HOSPITAL 5D 36

GENERAL ABBREVIATIONS

All. : Alley	**Est.** : Estate	**Lit.** : Little	**Sth.** : South
App. : Approach	**Fld.** : Field	**Lwr.** : Lower	**Sq.** : Square
Av. : Avenue	**Flds.** : Fields	**Mnr.** : Manor	**Sta.** : Station
Bungs. : Bungalows	**Gdns.** : Gardens	**Mdw.** : Meadow	**St.** : Street
Bus. : Business	**Gth.** : Garth	**Mdws.** : Meadows	**Ter.** : Terrace
Cen. : Centre	**Ga.** : Gate	**M.** : Mews	**Trad.** : Trading
Cl. : Close	**Gt.** : Great	**Mt.** : Mount	**Up.** : Upper
Comn. : Common	**Grn.** : Green	**Mus.** : Museum	**Va.** : Vale
Cnr. : Corner	**Gro.** : Grove	**Nth.** : North	**Vw.** : View
Cotts. : Cottages	**Hgts.** : Heights	**Pde.** : Parade	**Vs.** : Villas
Ct. : Court	**Ho.** : House	**Pk.** : Park	**Wlk.** : Walk
Cres. : Crescent	**Ind.** : Industrial	**Pl.** : Place	**W.** : West
Cft. : Croft	**Info.** : Information	**Ri.** : Rise	**Yd.** : Yard
Dr. : Drive	**Intl.** : International	**Rd.** : Road	
E. : East	**Junc.** : Junction	**Rdbt.** : Roundabout	
Ent. : Enterprise	**La.** : Lane	**Shop.** : Shopping	

LOCALITY ABBREVIATIONS

Abb A : **Abbotts Ann**	Elli : **Ellisfield**	Nat S : **Nately Scures**	Sman : **Smannell**
A'ver : **Andover**	Enh A : **Enham Alamein**	Newf : **Newfound**	S War : **South Warnborough**
And D : **Andover Down**	Far W : **Farleigh Wallop**	Newn : **Newnham**	Stev : **Steventon**
A'ell : **Andwell**	Free : **Freefolk**	Nth W : **North Waltham**	Stra S : **Stratfield Saye**
An V : **Anna Valley**	G Cla : **Goodworth Clatford**	N War : **North Warnborough**	Stra T : **Stratfield Turgis**
Ashe : **Ashe**	Grey : **Greywell**	Oak : **Oakley**	Tun : **Tunworth**
B'toke : **Basingstoke**	H Wes : **Hartley Wespall**	Odi : **Odiham**	Up N : **Up Nately**
Bau : **Baughurst**	H Win : **Hartley Wintney**	Old Bas : **Old Basing**	Up C : **Upper Clatford**
Charl : **Charlton**	Haze : **Hazeley**	Over : **Overton**	Up Woott : **Upper Wootton**
Cha A : **Charter Alley**	Hoo : **Hook**	Pen C : **Penton Corner**	Up G : **Upton Grey**
Chin : **Chineham**	Hur P : **Hurstbourne Priors**	Pen M : **Penton Mewsey**	Wel : **Well**
Clid : **Cliddesden**	K Enh : **Knights Enham**	Pic P : **Picket Piece**	W Cor : **Weston Corbett**
Col H : **Cole Henley**	L'stoke : **Laverstoke**	Rams : **Ramsdell**	Wher : **Wherwell**
Dea : **Deane**	L Sut : **Long Sutton**	Red R : **Red Rice**	Whit : **Whitchurch**
Dogm : **Dogmersfield**	Lych : **Lychpit**	Roth : **Rotherwick**	Winchf : **Winchfield**
Dumm : **Dummer**	Mapl : **Mapledurwell**	Sher J : **Sherborne St John**	Winsl : **Winslade**
E Ant : **East Anton**	Matt : **Mattingley**	Sher L : **Sherfield on Loddon**	W Law : **Wootton St Lawrence**
	M She : **Monk Sherborne**	Sil : **Silchester**	Wort : **Worting**

A

Abbey Ct. RG24: B'toke 7C **8**
 SP10: A'ver 6E **36**
Abbey Rd. RG24: B'toke 1B **16**
Abbott Cl. RG22: B'toke 7J **15**
ABBOTTS ANN 3A **38**
Abbotts Cl. SP11: Abb A 3A **38**
Abbotts Hill SP11: Abb A 4A **38**
Above Town SP11: Up C 3D **38**
Achilles Cl. RG24: Chin 4H **9**
Acorn Cl. RG21: B'toke 4G **17**
Acre Ct. SP10: A'ver 6G **37**
Acre Path SP10: A'ver 6G **37**
Active Life Cen.
 Basingstoke 3A **16**
Acton Ho. RG24: B'toke 5A **16**
Adams Cl. RG29: N War 6B **20**
Addison Gdns. RG29: Odi 6E **20**
Adelaide Cl. SP10: A'ver 6G **37**

Admirals Way SP10: A'ver 6J **37**
Adrian Cl. RG27: H Win 3K **13**
Aghemund Cl. RG24: Chin 5G **9**
Agricola Wlk. SP10: A'ver 3G **37**
Ajax Cl. RG24: Chin 4H **9**
Alanbrooke Cl. RG27: H Win . . .2J **13**
Albany Rd. SP10: A'ver 6D **36**
Albert Yd. RG21: B'toke 5D **16**
Albion Pl. RG27: H Win 2J **13**
Aldermaston Rd.
 RG24: B'toke, Sher J 4K **7**
 RG26: M She 1K **7**
Aldermaston Rd. Rdbt.
 RG21: B'toke 1B **16**
Aldermaston Rd. Sth.
 RG21: B'toke 2B **16**
Alderney Av. RG22: B'toke 3H **23**
Alders Cl. RG21: B'toke 4F **17**
 (off The Moorings)
Alderwood RG24: Chin 5H **9**
Alderwood Dr. RG27: Hoo 6B **12**

Aldrin Cl. SP10: Charl 3D **36**
Aldworth Cres. RG22: B'toke . . .5A **16**
Alencon Ho. RG21: B'toke 4D **16**
 (off Alencon Link)
Alencon Link RG21: B'toke 4C **16**
 SP10: A'ver 5A **36**
Alexander Bell Cen.
 RG24: B'toke 4D **32**
Alexandra Rd. RG21: B'toke . . .4B **16**
 SP10: A'ver 6E **36**
Alexandra Ter. RG27: Sher L . . .6G **5**
 RG29: N War 5C **20**
 (off Bridge Rd.)
Alfred Gdns. SP10: A'ver 4E **36**
Allen Cl. RG21: B'toke 6B **16**
Allenmoor La. RG27: Roth 1J **11**
Allington Ri. RG27: Sher L 3J **9**
Alliston Way RG22: B'toke 6H **15**
 RG28: Whit 7C **30**
Allnutt Av. RG21: B'toke 4E **16**

Almerston Rd. RG24: Sher J 1I
Almond Cl. RG24: Old Bas 3J
Alpine Ct. RG22: B'toke 6G
Altona Gdns. SP10: A'ver 3E
Alton Rd.
 RG25: B'toke, Winsl 1E
 RG29: Odi, S War 7A
Amazon Cl. RG21: B'toke 5B
Amber Gdns. SP10: A'ver 6C
Ambleside Cl. RG22: B'toke 7G
Amport Cl. RG24: Lych 1J
Amport Rd. RG27: Sher L 3
Anchor Ct. RG21: B'toke 5D
 (off London S
Anchor Vw. SP11: Up C 3D
Anchor Yd. RG21: B'toke 5D
Andeferas Rd. SP10: A'ver 3E
ANDOVER 7F
Andover Down Rdbt.
 SP10: A'ver 6K
Andover Golf Course 1G

...ver Leisure Cen. 6F 37
...ver Mus. 6G 37
...ver Rd.
  RG23: Newf, Oak 6A 14
  RG25: Dea, Oak 3J 33
  RG28: Whit 7B 30
...ver Station (Rail) 6E 36
...OVER WAR MEMORIAL
  COMMUNITY HOSPITAL
  ....5D 36
...ew Cl. RG29: N War 6B 20
...ew's La. RG29: L Sut ...7F 29
...WELL 3D 18
...ell Drove RG27: A'ell 4E 18
...ell La. RG27: A'ell 4E 18
...l Mdws. RG29: Odi 6E 20
...ers Pl. RG21: B'toke 4F 17
  (off The Moorings)
...esey Cl. RG24: B'toke 6E 8
  SP10: A'ver 2F 39
...A VALLEY 2C 38
...ey Cl. RG21: B'toke 7C 16
...er Cl. RG21: B'toke 5B 16
...n Cl. RG23: Oak 1B 22
...n Lakes Nature Reserve
  ....4E 36
...n Mill Rd. SP10: A'ver 7F 37
...n Rd. SP10: A'ver 1F 39
...n Trad. Est. SP10: A'ver ..7F 37
...m Cl. RG22: B'toke 6H 15
...l Theatre, The 4D 16
...l Way RG26: B'ley 4C 4
...lonia Ho. SP10: A'ver ...7F 37
  (off Winchester Rd.)
...e Dene RG26: B'ley 5C 4
...legarth Cl. RG21: B'toke ..6E 16
...leton Dr.
  RG24: B'toke, Sher J ...6C 8
...eton M. SP10: A'ver 1G 39
...etree Cl. RG23: Oak 2B 22
...e Tree Gro. SP10: A'ver ..5C 36
...etree Mead RG27: Hoo ...7C 12
...e Way RG24: Old Bas ...4K 17
...ley Cl. SP10: A'ver 2E 38
...adrome
  Basingstoke 4J 15
...oretum, The RG25: Up G ..4F 27
...dia Cl. RG22: B'toke 6G 23
...ery Flds. RG29: Odi 6E 20
...glen Rd. RG28: Whit 6B 30
...wright Gate SP10: A'ver ..4A 36
...tt Dr. RG21: B'toke 2D 16
...strong Ri. SP10: Charl ...3D 36
...strong Rd. RG24: B'toke ..2G 17
...t Cl. RG22: B'toke 3K 23
...n Cl. RG23: Oak 7A 14
...w La. RG27: H Win 2H 13
...ur Ct. RG21: B'toke 4C 16
  (off Solby's Rd.)
...sts Way SP10: A'ver 4E 36
...n Ct. RG21: B'toke 4F 17
...ndel Gdns. RG23: B'toke ..2J 15
...ension Cl. RG24: B'toke ...7F 9
...E 3G 33
...e Cl. RG23: W Law 2E 14
...field RG24: Chin 5H 9
...field Rd. SP10: A'ver 6C 36
...Gro. RG24: Old Bas 3A 18
...lawn Gdns. SP10: A'ver ..1G 39
...lea RG27: Hoo 6B 12
...ley Gdns. RG23: Oak 7B 14
...ley Lodge RG21: B'toke ...6C 16
  (off Winchester Rd.)
...moor La. RG24: Old Bas ..3A 18
...l Tree Cl. RG23: Oak 2A 22
...Tree Rd. SP10: A'ver 6B 36
...wood RG24: Chin 6G 9
...wood Way RG23: B'toke ...2K 15
...wood Way Rdbt.
  RG23: B'toke 2K 15
...en Cl. RG27: Hoo 6B 12
...en Ho. RG24: Old Bas ...4B 18
...en Way RG21: B'toke 2E 16
...ire Pl. RG24: B'toke 7F 9
...r Ct. SP10: A'ver 1C 38
  (off Floral Way)
...r Rd. RG22: B'toke 3G 23
...oke Cft. RG27: Hoo 7D 12
...oll Cl. SP10: A'ver 3F 37
...oll, The RG24: B'toke 7F 9
...wood Cl. RG21: B'toke ...5B 16

Attwood Cl. Mobile Home Pk.
  RG21: B'toke 5B 16
Augusta Way Central
  SP11: E Ant 2H 37
Augusta Way East
  SP11: E Ant 2H 37
Augusta Way West
  SP11: E Ant 3H 37
Augustine Way SP10: Charl ..3C 36
Augustus Dr. RG23: B'toke ..2J 15
Augustus Wlk. SP10: A'ver ..3G 37
Auklet Cl. RG22: B'toke 3F 23
Aurora Dr. RG22: B'toke 6G 23
Austen Gro. RG22: B'toke ...7A 16
Avenue, The RG25: B'toke ...2G 25
  RG25: Far W 7K 23
Avenue Cl. RG22: B'toke 6D 36
Avenue Cl. SP10: A'ver 6D 36
Aviary Cl. RG22: B'toke 1G 17
Aviemore Dr. RG23: Oak 1A 22
Avington Way RG27: Sher L ..3J 9
Avon Cl. SP10: A'ver 4H 37
Avon Rd. RG23: Oak 1B 22
Avon Wlk. RG21: B'toke 4F 17
Ayliffe Ho. RG22: B'toke 5K 15
Aylings Cl. RG23: Wort 4H 15
Aylwin Cl. RG21: B'toke 7C 16
Azalea Ct. SP10: A'ver 1C 38

B

Bach Cl. RG22: B'toke 3K 23
Baden Gdns. RG23: B'toke ..2K 15
Badgers Bank RG24: Lych ..1H 17
Bagwell La. RG27: Winchf ...2J 21
  RG29: Odi 4G 21
Baird Av. RG22: B'toke 7A 16
Bakers Yd. RG23: Oak 2B 22
Balksbury Hill Ind. Est.
  SP11: Up C 2D 38
Balksbury Hill SP11: Up C ...2D 38
Ballard Cl. RG22: B'toke 6J 15
Balmoral Ct. RG22: B'toke ...6J 15
  SP10: A'ver 6F 37
Balmoral Rd. SP10: A'ver ...6F 37
Balmoral Way RG22: B'toke ..6J 15
Balsan Cl. RG24: B'toke 1J 15
Banbury Way RG22: B'toke ...7C 8
Band Hall Pl. RG27: Hoo 7B 12
Banks Cl. SP10: A'ver 7D 36
Barbel Av. RG21: B'toke 4F 17
Barber Rd. RG22: B'toke 2K 23
Barbour Cl. RG29: Odi 2C 28
Barcelona Cl. SP10: A'ver ...5G 37
Bardwell Cl. RG22: B'toke ...5J 15
Baredown, The RG27: Nat S ..2H 19
Barley Rd. SP11: E Ant 2H 37
Barley Vw. RG25: Nth W ...2D 34
Barlows La. SP10: A'ver 2E 38
Barnfield Rd. SP10: A'ver ...1D 38
Barn La. RG23: Oak 2A 22
Barns, The RG25: Dumm ...3H 35
Barnwells Ct. RG27: H Win ..1K 13
Barracks, The RG27: Hoo ...1H 19
Barra Cl. RG23: Oak 7A 14
Barrett Ct. RG21: B'toke 7E 16
Barrington Dr. RG24: B'toke ..6D 8
Barron Pl. RG24: B'toke 1H 15
Barrow Cl. RG21: B'toke 7E 16
BARROWFIELD SP11: G Cla ..6E 38
BARROW HILL 7E 38
Barrow Hill SP11: G Cla 7D 38
Barry Way RG22: B'toke 3K 23
Bartlett Cl. RG26: B'ley 5E 4
Bartlett Ct. RG27: Hoo 7B 12
Bartley Point RG27: Hoo 1B 20
Bartley Way RG27: Hoo 1C 20
Bartley Wood Bus. Pk. (East)
  RG27: Hoo 1C 20
Bartley Wood Bus. Pk. (West)
  RG27: Hoo 1B 20
Bartok Cl. RG22: B'toke 1A 24
Barton Cl. SP10: Charl 3C 36
Barton's Ct. RG29: Odi 6D 20
Barton's La. RG24: Old Bas ..2H 17
Basepoint Business &
  Innovation Cen.
  SP10: A'ver 4C 36
Basepoint Ent. Cen.
  RG24: B'toke 1G 17

Basingfield Cl.
  RG24: Old Bas 5K 17
Basing House
  Barton's La. 2J 17
  Musket Copse 3J 17
Basing Rd. RG24: Old Bas ...3G 17
BASINGSTOKE & 4D 16
BASINGSTOKE &
  NORTH HAMPSHIRE
  HOSPITAL 1A 16
Basingstoke Bus. Cen.
  RG22: B'toke 7A 16
Basingstoke Crematorium
  RG25: Nth W 4A 34
Basingstoke Ent. Cen.
  RG22: Wort 5H 15
Basingstoke Golf Cen. 5J 15
Basingstoke Golf Course 5F 23
Basingstoke Leisure Pk.
  RG22: B'toke 4K 15
Basingstoke Rd.
  RG26: Rams, Up Woott ...1E 6
  RG22: B'toke 3H 23
Basingstoke Station (Rail) ...3D 16
Basingstoke Town FC
  (The Camrose) 7A 16
Basing Vw. RG21: B'toke 4E 16
Basswood Dr. RG24: B'toke ..1K 15
Batchelor Dr. RG24: Old Bas ..4A 18
Batchelor's Barn Rd.
  SP10: A'ver 6H 37
Battens Av. RG25: Over 3D 32
Battledown Cotts.
  RG23: Wort 1E 22
Baughurst Rd.
  RG26: Bau, Rams 1D 6
Baynard Cl. RG21: B'toke ...2E 16
Bay Tree Way RG21: B'toke ..2E 16
Beach Piece Way
  RG22: B'toke 3H 23
Beaconsfield Rd.
  RG21: B'toke 5D 16
Beales Cl. SP10: A'ver 6G 37
Beal's Pightle RG26: Cha A ..1F 7
Bear Ct. RG24: B'toke 2H 17
Beatty Ct. SP10: A'ver 6J 37
Beauclerk Grn.
  RG27: Winchf 7J 13
Beaulieu Ct. RG21: B'toke ...4F 17
  (off Loddon Dr.)
  SP10: A'ver 4H 37
  (off River Way)
Beaumaris Ct. SP10: A'ver ...1D 38
Beaurepaire Cl. RG26: B'ley ..4A 4
Becket Ct. RG23: Wort 5G 15
Beckett Cl. RG23: Wort 4G 15
Beckett Gdns. RG26: B'ley ...5C 4
Beckett Rd. SP10: A'ver 5D 36
Becketts RG27: H Win 2J 13
Beddington Ct. RG24: Lych ..1J 17
Bede Dr. SP10: Charl 3C 36
Bedford Wlk. RG21: B'toke ..4D 16
  (off Festival Pl.)
Bedser Sq. SP10: A'ver 6H 37
Beecham Berry
  RG22: B'toke 3K 23
Beech Cl. RG25: Over 1D 32
Beech Cl. RG28: Whit 5C 30
Beechcrest Vw.
  RG27: Hoo 6B 12
Beechcroft Cl. SP10: A'ver ..5F 37
Beechdown Health and
  Leisure Club 1J 23
Beechdown Ho.
  RG22: B'toke 1J 23
Beech Dr. RG24: Chin 5J 9
Beeches, The RG22: B'toke ..4K 23
  SP10: A'ver 6D 36
Beech Lodge RG27: H Win ..2K 13
Beech Tree Cl. RG23: Oak ...2A 22
Beech Wlk. SP10: A'ver 7C 36
Beech Way RG23: B'toke ...2J 15
Beechwood RG24: Chin 5G 9
Beechwood Cl. RG24: B'toke ..4J 23
Beethoven Rd. RG22: B'toke ..1A 24
BEGGARWOOD 5G 23
Beggarwood La.
  RG22: B'toke 5F 23
Begonia Cl. RG22: B'toke ...3G 23
Belfry Sq. RG22: B'toke 5G 23
Belgrave M. RG27: H Win ...2K 13

Bellevue RG28: Whit 6C 30
Belle Vue Rd.
  RG24: Old Bas 3K 17
  SP10: A'ver 1G 39
Bell Mdw. Rd. RG27: Hoo ...7B 12
Bell M. RG28: Whit 6C 30
Bell Rd. RG24: B'toke 2G 17
  SP10: A'ver 6H 37
Bell St. RG28: Whit 6C 30
Bell Yd. RG28: Whit 6C 30
Belmont Cl. SP10: A'ver 1G 39
Belmont Hgts. RG22: B'toke ..5J 23
Belmont Rd. SP10: A'ver 1G 39
Beltex Wlk. SP11: E Ant 2H 37
  (off Romney Rd.)
Belvedere Gdns. RG24: Chin ..4J 9
Belverdere Ho. RG21: B'toke ..3F 17
Benbow Ct. SP10: A'ver 6J 37
Benford Ct. RG29: Odi 7E 20
  (off Buryfields)
Benham Rd. RG24: B'toke ...6C 8
Bennet Cl. RG21: B'toke 2E 16
Bentall Pl. SP10: A'ver 7F 37
Benwell Cl. RG29: Odi 2C 28
BERE HILL
  RG28 ....5D 30
  SP10 ....1G 39
Bere Hill RG28: Whit 5D 30
Bere Hill Cl. RG28: Whit 5D 30
Bere Hill Cres. SP10: A'ver ..7H 37
Bere Hill Pk. (Caravan Pk.)
  RG28: Whit 5D 30
Beresford Centre, The
  RG24: B'toke 1G 17
Beresford Cl. SP10: A'ver ...2F 39
Beresford Ga. SP10: A'ver ...5K 37
Berewyk Cl. RG22: B'toke ...3G 23
Berkeley Dr. RG22: B'toke ...2B 24
Bermuda Cl. RG24: B'toke ...6E 8
Bernstein Rd. RG22: B'toke ..3J 23
  (not continuous)
Berrington Way
  RG24: B'toke 1G 17
Berry Ct. RG27: Hoo 1A 20
Berrydown La. RG25: Over ...4E 32
Berry Way RG22: B'toke 7B 36
Berwyn Cl. RG22: B'toke ...6G 15
Bessemer Pk. RG22: B'toke ..7B 16
Bessemer Rd. RG21: B'toke ..7B 16
Beverley Cl. RG22: B'toke ...1D 24
Bexmoor RG24: Old Bas 3J 17
Bexmoor Way
  RG24: Old Bas 3J 17
Bible Flds. RG25: Dumm ...3G 35
Bicester Cl. RG28: Whit 6C 30
BIDDEN 3H 27
Bidden Rd. RG25: Up G 5F 27
  RG29: N War 1K 27
Bilbao Cl. SP10: A'ver 5J 37
Bilton Ind. Est. RG24: B'toke ..7G 9
Bilton Rd. RG24: B'toke 7G 9
Binfields Cl. RG24: Chin 7H 9
Binfields Farm La.
  RG24: Old Bas 7J 9
Binfields Rdbt. RG24: Chin ..7H 9
Bingley Cl. RG21: B'toke 2E 16
Birches Crest RG22: B'toke ..4K 23
Birch Gro. RG27: Hoo 6B 12
Birchwood RG24: Chin 5H 9
Bishop's Way SP10: A'ver ...6E 36
Bittern Cl. RG22: B'toke 2F 23
Blackberry Wlk. RG24: Lych ..2G 17
Blackbird Cl. RG22: B'toke ...2F 23
Blackbird Ct. SP10: A'ver ...3G 37
BLACK DAM 6F 17
Black Dam Cen.
  RG21: B'toke 6F 17
Black Dam Nature Reserve ..5H 17
Black Dam Rdbt.
  RG21: B'toke 5G 17
Black Dam Way
  RG21: B'toke 6F 17
Blackdown Cl. RG22: B'toke ..6H 15
Blacksmiths Rdbt.
  SP10: A'ver 5G 37
Blackstocks La.
  RG27: Nat S, Up N 4F 19
Black Swan Yd. SP10: A'ver ..6G 37
  (off East St.)
Blackthorn Way
  RG23: B'toke 3J 15

Blackwater Cl. RG21: B'toke ...4E 16
RG23: Oak 1B 22
Blaegrove La. RG27: Up N 5F 19
Blair Rd. RG21: B'toke 6C 16
Blake Cl. RG29: Odi 2C 28
Blake Ct. SP10: A'ver 5F 37
Blendon Dr. SP10: A'ver 5C 36
Blenheim Ct. RG21: B'toke ...4B 16
Blenheim Rd.
      RG24: Old Bas 4A 18
Bliss Cl. RG22: B'toke 1A 24
Blossom Cl. RG27: H Win 7B 36
Bloswood Dr. RG28: Whit 6B 30
Bloswood La.
      RG28: Hur P, Whit 3A 30
Bluebell Cl. SP10: A'ver 7B 36
Blueberry Gdns. SP10: A'ver ..7B 36
Bluehaven Wlk. RG27: Hoo ...7K 11
Blue Hayes Cl. SP10: A'ver ...7F 37
Blunden Cl. RG21: B'toke 1C 24
Blunt Rd. RG22: B'toke 6F 23
Bodmin Cl. RG22: B'toke 6H 15
Bolton Cres. RG22: B'toke 6A 16
Bond Cl. RG22: B'toke 1G 17
Boon Way RG23: Oak 7A 14
Borden Gates SP10: A'ver 7F 37
Boreway Cl. SP11: E Ant 2J 37
Borkum Cl. SP10: A'ver 3E 36
Borodin Cl. RG22: B'toke 2B 24
Borough Ct. Rd.
      RG27: H Win 5E 12
Borsberry Cl. SP10: A'ver 6G 37
Boscowen Cl. SP10: A'ver 6J 37
      (off Admirals Way)
Bottle La. RG27: Matt 1A 12
Boulter Cres. SP11: A'ver 7K 37
Boulter Rd. SP11: A'ver 7K 37
Bounty Ri. RG21: B'toke 5C 16
Bounty Rd. RG21: B'toke 5C 16
Bourdillon Gdns.
      RG24: B'toke 7E 8
Bourne Ct. RG21: B'toke 4F 17
      SP10: A'ver 4H 37
      (off River Way)
Bourne Fld. RG24: Sher J 4A 8
Bow Fld. RG27: Hoo 7C 12
Bow Gdns. RG27: Sher L 7G 5
Bow Gro. RG27: Sher L 6G 5
Bowling Grn. Dr. RG27: Hoo ..7K 11
Bowlplex
      Basingstoke 4J 15
Bowman Rd. RG24: Chin 4H 9
Bowyer Cl. RG21: B'toke 5C 16
Boyce Cl. RG22: B'toke 2J 23
Bracher Cl. SP10: A'ver 6G 37
Bracken Bank RG24: Lych ...1H 17
Brackenbury SP10: A'ver 5C 36
Brackens, The RG22: B'toke ..4J 23
Brackley Av. RG27: H Win ...2H 13
Brackley Way RG22: B'toke ..1J 23
Bracknell La.
      RG27: H Win, Haze 1H 13
Bradbury Cl. RG28: Whit 6B 30
Bradman Sq. SP10: A'ver 3H 37
      (off Cricketers Way)
Bradwell Cl. SP10: Charl 3C 36
Braemar Dr. RG23: Oak 7A 14
Brahms Rd. RG22: B'toke 2A 24
Braine L'Alleud Rd.
      RG21: B'toke 3D 16
Bramble Wlk. SP11: E Ant ...4H 37
Bramble Way RG24: Old Bas ..3A 18
Brambling Cl. RG22: B'toke ..3F 23
Bramblys Cl. RG21: B'toke ...5C 16
Bramblys Dr. RG21: B'toke ...5C 16
Bramdown Hgts.
      RG22: B'toke 4H 23
BRAMLEY 4C 4
BRAMLEY GREEN 5D 4
Bramley Grn. Rd.
      RG26: B'ley 5D 4
Bramley La. RG26: B'ley 3C 4
Bramley Rd. RG7: Sil 1A 4
      RG26: B'ley 1A 4
      RG27: Sher L 6G 5
Bramley Station (Rail) 4C 4
Brampton Gdns.
      RG22: B'toke 5H 23
Bramshott Dr. RG27: Hoo 7B 12
Brancaster Av. SP10: Charl ...3C 36

Bransbury Gro. RG27: Sher L ...3J 9
Branton Cl. RG22: B'toke 6J 15
Breach Gdns. RG27: Sher L ...7H 5
Breach La. RG27: Sher L 7H 5
Breadels Ct. RG22: B'toke ...6H 23
Breadels Fld. RG22: B'toke ...6G 23
Bremen Gdns. SP10: A'ver 4E 36
Brewer Cl. RG22: B'toke 6J 15
Brew Ho. La. RG27: H Win ...2K 13
Briars Cft. SP10: A'ver 7F 37
Brickfields Cl. RG24: Lych 1H 17
Bridge Rd. RG29: N War 5C 20
Bridge St. RG25: Over 3C 32
      SP10: A'ver 7F 37
BRIGHTON HILL 2K 23
Brighton Hill Cen.
      RG22: B'toke 2K 23
Brighton Hill Pde.
      RG22: B'toke 2K 23
Brighton Hill Retail Pk.
      ....7A 16
Brighton Hill Rdbt.
      RG22: B'toke 7A 16
Brighton Way RG22: B'toke ..2K 23
Britannia Dr. RG22: B'toke ...6G 23
Britten Rd. RG22: B'toke 1A 24
Broadhurst Gro. RG24: Lych ..2H 17
Broad Leaze RG27: Hoo 6A 12
BROADMERE 7A 24
Broadmere Rd.
      RG25: Far W 7A 24
Broadmere Rd.
      ....5G 23
BROAD OAK 5G 21
Broad Oak La. RG29: Odi 6G 21
Broad Wlk. RG25: B'toke 2G 25
Broadway RG28: Whit 7D 30
Broadway, The SP10: A'ver ...7F 37
      (off Western Rd.)
Brocas Dr. RG21: B'toke 2E 16
Bromelia Cl. RG26: B'ley 3C 4
Bronze Cl. RG22: B'toke 6G 23
Brooke Dr. SP10: A'ver 5D 36
Brookfield Cl. RG24: Chin 5J 9
Brookham Grange
      RG27: Sher L 3J 9
Brooks Cl. RG28: Whit 7D 30
Brooks Ri. SP10: A'ver 5D 36
Brookvale Cl. RG21: B'toke ...4C 16
Brookvale School
      RG21: B'toke 4B 16
Brook Way SP11: An V 3B 38
Brown Cft. RG27: Hoo 7K 11
Browning Cl. RG24: B'toke ...1E 16
Browns Cl. RG26: B'ley 3C 4
Brunel Gate SP10: A'ver 4A 36
Brunel Rd. RG21: B'toke 3A 16
Brunswick Pl. RG21: B'toke ..1B 24
Buckby La. RG21: B'toke 4F 17
Buckfast Cl. RG24: B'toke ...7C 8
Buckingham Ct.
      ....1G 23
Buckingham Pde.
      ....1G 23
Buckland Av. RG22: B'toke ...1K 23
Buckland Mill RG27: Hoo 1J 19
Buckland Pde. RG22: B'toke ..7K 15
Buckland Ter. RG27: Sher L ...3J 9
BUCKSKIN 6G 15
Budd's Cl. RG21: B'toke 5C 16
Buffins Cnr. RG29: Odi 7C 20
Buffins Rd. RG29: Odi 7C 20
Bufton Fld. RG29: N War 6C 20
Bulls Bushes RG27: Hoo 1K 19
Bullsdown Cl. RG27: Sher L ...6F 5
Bunnian Pl. RG21: B'toke 3D 16
Bunting M. RG22: B'toke 3F 23
Burberry Ho. RG27: Hoo 7A 12
Burdock Cl. SP11: G Cla 7E 38
Burgage Fld. RG28: Whit 5D 30
Burgate Cres. RG27: Sher L ..3K 9
Burgess Cl. RG29: Odi 7C 20
Burgess Rd. RG21: B'toke ...3C 16
Burghfield Wlk. RG22: Wort ..6G 15
Burkal Dr. RG21: B'toke 2F 37
Burley La. RG25: Ashe 7G 33
Burlingham Grange
      RG29: N War 6C 20
Burnaby Cl. RG26: B'ley 6J 15
Burnhams Cl. SP10: A'ver 3F 37
Burns Cl. RG24: B'toke 1E 16

Burrowfields RG22: B'toke 5H 23
Burton's Gdns.
      RG24: Old Bas 2K 17
BURY, THE 7E 20
Bury, The RG29: Odi 6E 20
Burydown Mead
      RG25: Nth W 2D 34
Buryfields RG29: Odi 7E 20
Bury Hill Cl. SP11: An V 3C 38
Bury Rd. RG23: B'toke 3K 15
Butler Cl. RG22: B'toke 5J 15
Buttermere Dr. RG22: B'toke ..1G 23
Butts Mdw. RG27: Hoo 7A 12
Butty, The RG21: B'toke 4F 17
Byfleet Av. RG24: Old Bas ...3K 17
Byng Wlk. SP10: A'ver 6J 37
Byrd Gdns. RG22: B'toke 3J 23
Byron Cl. RG24: B'toke 7F 9

C

Cadnam Cl. RG23: Oak 7B 14
Caerleon Dr. RG23: B'toke ...2F 37
Caernarvon Cl. RG23: B'toke ..4J 15
Caesar Cl. RG23: B'toke 2J 15
      (off Augustus Dr.)
      SP10: A'ver 3G 37
Caesar's Way RG28: Whit 5B 30
Cairngorm Cl. RG22: B'toke ..5H 15
Caithness Cl. RG23: Oak 1A 22
Calder Ct. SP10: A'ver 4H 37
Calleva Cl. RG22: B'toke 3H 23
Camberry Cl. RG21: B'toke ...6E 16
Cambrian Way RG22: B'toke ..6H 15
Camelot Cl. SP10: A'ver 4F 37
Camfield Cl. RG21: B'toke ...6E 16
Camford Cl. RG22: B'toke 6G 23
Camlea Cl. RG21: B'toke 6E 16
Campbell Ct. RG26: B'ley 5E 4
Campbell Rd. RG26: B'ley 5E 4
Campion Way RG27: H Win ..1K 13
Campsie Cl. RG22: B'toke 5H 15
Camrose Way RG21: B'toke ..7E 16
Cam Wlk. RG22: B'toke 4F 17
Camwood Cl. RG21: B'toke ...6E 16
Canadian Way RG24: B'toke ..1J 15
Canal Cl. RG29: N War 5C 20
Canal Reach RG27: A'ell 4D 18
Canberra Way RG27: Sher L ..6G 23
Candover Ct. RG22: B'toke ...5F 23
Cannock Ct. RG22: B'toke 5J 15
Canterbury Cl. RG22: B'toke ..2H 23
Carbonel Cl. RG23: Wort 4G 15
Cardinal M. SP10: A'ver 6F 37
Carisbrooke Cl.
      RG23: B'toke 1G 23
Carleton Cl. RG27: Hoo 7K 11
Carlisle Cl. RG23: B'toke 3J 15
Carmichael Way
      RG22: B'toke 2J 23
Carpenters Cl. RG27: Sher L ..6G 5
Carpenters Cl. RG22: B'toke ..7K 15
Carpenter's Down
      RG24: B'toke 7D 8
Cartel Bus Cen.
      ....1G 17
Carter Dr. RG24: B'toke 6C 8
Carters Mdw. SP10: Charl 4C 36
Castle Fld. Path
      ....6D 16
Castle Ri. RG29: N War 5C 20
Castle Rd. RG21: B'toke 6D 16
Castle Sq. RG21: B'toke 5D 16
Caston's Wlk. RG21: B'toke ..5D 16
Caston's Yd. RG21: B'toke ...5D 16
Catkin Cl. RG24: Chin 5H 9
Cattle La. SP11: Abb A 3A 38
Causeway Cotts.
      RG27: H Win 2K 13
Causton Rd. RG22: B'toke ...6H 23
Cavalier Cl. RG24: Old Bas ...3A 18
Cavalier Rd. RG24: Old Bas ..3A 18
Cavell Cl. RG24: Lych 1J 17
Caxton Cl. SP10: A'ver 5B 36
Cayman Cl. RG24: B'toke 7F 9
Cedar Ter. RG27: H Win 3H 13
Cedar Tree Cl. RG23: Oak ...2A 22
Cedar Wlk. SP10: A'ver 7C 36
Cedar Way RG23: B'toke 2K 15
Cedarwood RG24: Chin 5F 9

Cedarwood Pl. SP10: A'ver ...6.
Celtic Dr. SP10: A'ver 1C
Cemetery Hill RG29: Odi 7H
Cemetery La. RG25: Up G 5F
Central Studio (Theatre) 6E
Central Way SP10: A'ver 5H
Centre Court Tennis Cen. 2
Centre Dr. RG24: Chin 2
Centurion Way RG22: B'toke ..3H
      (not continue
Century Cl. RG25: Clid 3C
Chaffers Cl. RG29: L Sut 7C
Chaffinch Cl. RG22: B'toke ...2G
Chaldon Grn. RG24: Lych ....1.
Chalk Va. RG24: Old Bas 4A
Chalky Copse RG27: Hoo 6A
Challis Cl. RG22: B'toke 7
Challoner Cl. RG22: B'toke ...6
Chandler Rd. RG21: B'toke ...7C
Chantry Centre, The
      SP10: A'ver 6E
Chantry Cl. RG27: Hoo 1A
Chantry M. RG22: B'toke 3
Chantry St. SP10: A'ver 6E
Chantry Way RG22: B'toke ...6E
Chapel Cl. RG24: Old Bas ...2K
      RG25: Dumm 2H
Chapel Hill RG21: B'toke 3C
Chapel Pond Dr.
      RG29: N War 6C
Chapel River Cl.
      SP10: A'ver 7C
Chapel Row RG27: H Win ...1K
Chapel St. RG25: Nth W 2C
Chapel Wlk. RG25: Clid 3C
Chapter Ter. RG27: H Win ...1K
Charlbury La. RG24: B'toke ...7
Charlcot RG28: Whit 7C
Charledown Cl. RG25: Over ..4C
Charledown Rd.
      RG25: Over ....7.
Charles Cl. RG27: Hoo 7A
Charles Dalton Ct.
      SP10: A'ver 7C
Charles Richards Cl.
      RG21: B'toke 6C
Charles St. RG22: B'toke 5K
Charlotte Cl. SP10: A'ver 4D
CHARLTON 4D
Charlton Leisure Cen. 4B
Charlton Pl. SP10: A'ver 4D
Charlton Rd. SP10: A'ver 4D
      (not continue
Charlton Rdbt. SP10: A'ver ...4D
Charlton Sports & Leisure Cen.
      ....3B
Charnwood Cl. RG22: B'toke ..6H
      SP10: A'ver 1G
CHARTER ALLEY ....1.
Chatsworth Cl. SP10: A'ver ...7D
Chatsworth Grn.
      RG22: B'toke 4J
Chatter La. RG28: Whit 6C
Chaucer Av. SP10: A'ver 5C
Chaucer Cl. RG24: B'toke ....7.
Cheavley Cl. SP10: A'ver 6B
Chelmer Cl. RG21: B'toke 4F
      (off Loddon
Chelsea Ho. RG21: B'toke ....4.
      (off Festival
Chequers Rd. RG21: B'toke ...4E
Cherry Cl. RG27: Hoo 6B
Cherry Orchard SP10: A'ver ..6B
Cherry Tree Rd. SP10: A'ver ..5D
Cherry Tree Wlk.
      RG21: B'toke 1E
Cherrywood RG24: Chin 5H
Chesterfield Rd.
      RG21: B'toke 6E
Chester Pl. RG21: B'toke 5C
Chestnut Av. SP10: A'ver 2E
Chestnut Bank
      RG24: Old Bas 2K
Cheviot Cl. RG22: B'toke 2K
Cheviot Rd. SP11: E Ant 2H
Chichester Cl. RG24: B'toke ..7A
Chichester Pl. RG22: B'toke ..7C
Chilcomb Cl. RG24: Chin 6G
Chilton Ridge RG22: B'toke ...6E
Chilworth Way RG27: Sher L ..3J
CHINEHAM 5

ham Bus. Pk.
RG24: Chin 4G 9
ham La. RG24: B'toke 1E 16
RG24: B'toke, Sher J 6B 8
ham Pk. Ct.
RG24: B'toke 1F 17
ham Shop. Cen.
RG24: Chin 7H 9
enham Cl. RG22: Wort . . .5G 15
rs Cl. RG22: B'toke 6J 15
n Rd. RG22: B'toke 2K 23
h Cl. SP10: A'ver 6G 37
CH END 2A 10
h Farm Cl.
RG25: Nth W 1C 34
hill Av. RG29: Odi 1D 28
hill Cl. RG27: H Win 1H 13
RG29: Odi 2D 28
hill Plaza RG21: B'toke . . .4E 16
hill Way RG21: B'toke . . .4D 16
SP10: A'ver 5G 37
hill Way E.
RG21: B'toke 4E 16
hill Way W.
RG21: B'toke 4A 16
RG22: B'toke 4K 15
SP10: A'ver 6A 36
h Lands RG26: B'ley 4A 4
h La. RG21: B'toke 4D 16
RG23: Wort 5G 15
RG24: Old Bas 3K 17
RG25: Clid 3C 24
RG27: H Win 4K 13
SP11: G Cla 6F 39
SP11: Up C 4E 38
h M. SP11: An V 3B 38
h Path RG24: Sher J 4A 8
RG27: Hoo 1K 19
RG27: Newn 7G 11
h Rd. RG25: Nth W 2C 34
RG25: Over 3C 32
h Sq. RG21: B'toke 4D 16
h St. RG21: B'toke 4D 16
(not continuous)
RG25: Up G 5F 27
RG28: Whit 7B 30
RG29: Odi 6D 20
(not continuous)
h Vw. RG27: H Win 4J 13
RG27: Hoo 7B 12
RG29: S War 7K 27
SP11: Up C 3D 38
ons Rd. RG24: Chin 5H 9
Wall Ho. RG21: B'toke 3F 17
ville Ri. RG27: Sher L 3J 9
bers Farm Rd. RG7: Sil . . .1A 4
ndon Av. SP10: A'ver 1D 38
M. RG28: Whit 7C 30
ord Mnr. SP11: Up C 3D 38
dius Cl. SP10: A'ver 2G 37
dius Dr. RG23: B'toke 2J 15
horpe Rd. RG22: B'toke . . .6J 15
on Cl. RG27: H Win 3J 13
ver Rd. RG22: B'toke 6J 15
re Rd. RG24: B'toke 6D 8
ents Gdns. RG28: Whit . . .6C 30
ers Cl. RG24: Chin 6H 9
edge Way RG29: N War . . .5C 20
eland Cl. RG22: B'toke . . .6H 15
es La. RG25: Up G 4F 27
DESDEN 3C 24
esden Cl. RG21: B'toke . . .7D 16
esden La.
RG22: B'toke 5H 23
esden Rd.
RG21: B'toke 7D 16
(not continuous)
n Ter. RG21: B'toke 3D 16
n Wlk. RG21: B'toke 4D 16
(off Festival Pl.)
ters, The SP10: A'ver 6F 37
e, The RG23: B'toke 2K 15
RG26: M She 2H 7
RG29: Odi 7D 20
er Fld. RG24: Lych 2H 17
er Leaf Way
RG24: Old Bas 5K 17

Clover M. SP10: A'ver 7G 37
Clyde Ct. SP10: A'ver 4H 37
Coachways SP10: A'ver . . .1F 39
Coates Cl. RG22: B'toke . . .1B 24
Cobb Dr. RG21: E Ant 2H 37
Cobbett Grn. RG22: B'toke .7A 16
Colbred Wlk. SP11: E Ant . . .2J 37
Coldharbour RG25: Nth W . . .2C 34
Cold Harbour Cotts.
RG25: Clid 3B 24
Cold Harbour Ct.
SP10: A'ver 7G 37
Colebrook Way SP10: A'ver . .7C 36
Cole Cl. SP10: A'ver 2F 37
COLE HENLEY 1D 30
Coleman Cl. RG21: B'toke . .2E 16
Colenzo Dr. SP10: A'ver . . .5G 37
College M. SP10: A'ver 6F 37
College Rd. RG21: B'toke . . .4B 16
Collingwood Wlk.
SP10: A'ver 6J 37
Collins Cl. SP10: Charl 3D 36
Colne Way RG21: B'toke . . .4F 17
COLT HILL 6F 21
Coltsfoot Pl. RG27: Hoo . . .6C 12
Columbine Rd.
RG22: B'toke 3G 23
Columbus Way SP10: A'ver . .5K 37
Colvin Cl. SP10: A'ver 7G 37
Colyer Cl. RG22: B'toke . . .6J 15
Compass Fld. RG27: Hoo . . .7B 12
Compton Cl. RG27: Hoo . . .7B 12
Compton Sq. SP10: A'ver . . .3H 37
Compton Way RG27: Sher L . .3K 9
Conholt Rd. SP10: A'ver . . .2F 39
Coniston Rd. RG22: B'toke . .1G 23
Constable Cl. RG21: B'toke . .6F 17
Constable Ct. SP10: A'ver . . .5F 37
Constantine Sq. SP10: A'ver . .3H 37
(off Cricketers Way)
Constantine Way
RG22: B'toke 4G 23
Coombehurst Dr.
RG21: B'toke 7D 16
Coopers Ct. RG26: B'ley 4C 4
Coopers La. RG26: B'ley 4B 4
Coop La. RG27: A'ell 3E 18
Copland Ct. RG22: B'toke . . .2J 23
Coppice M. RG23: B'toke . . .3J 15
Coppice Pale RG24: Old Bas . .6D 8
Copse, The RG23: Dumm . . .7D 22
Copse Caravan Site, The
RG23: Dumm 7D 22
Copse La. RG24: Lych 1J 17
Copse La. RG29: L Sut 7D 28
Copse Rd. RG25: Over 1D 32
Copse Vw. Cl. RG24: Chin . . .5H 9
Cordale Rd. RG21: B'toke . . .6C 16
Corelli Rd. RG22: B'toke . . .2B 24
Corfe Wlk. RG23: B'toke . . .3J 15
Corinthian Cl. RG22: B'toke . .3H 23
SP10: A'ver 3G 37
Cormorant Cl. RG22: B'toke . .2F 23
Cornfields SP10: A'ver 1H 39
Cornfields, The
RG22: B'toke 3J 23
Cornish Cl. RG22: B'toke . . .6J 15
Coronation Cl. RG29: Odi . . .6E 20
Coronation Cotts.
RG23: W Law 2E 14
Coronation Rd. RG21: B'toke . .3E 16
Corunna Main SP10: A'ver . .6G 37
Cotswold Cl. RG22: B'toke . .5H 15
Cottage Grn. RG27: H Win . .3K 13
SP11: G Cla 7E 38
Cottle Cl. RG21: B'toke 7C 16
Council Rd. RG21: B'toke . . .5D 16
COUNTESS OF BRECKNOCK HOUSE
(HOSPICE) 5D 36
Court Drove RG25: Over . . .1B 32
Courtyard, The RG22: B'toke . .5G 23
Coventry Cl. RG22: B'toke . .2H 23
Cowdery Hgts.
RG24: Old Bas 3G 17
COW DOWN 2K 39
Cowdown La.
SP11: A'ver, G Cla 4G 39
Cowdrey Sq. SP10: A'ver . . .3G 37
Cowfold La.
RG27: Matt, Roth 2K 11
Cowslad Dr. RG24: Old Bas . .6J 9

Cowslip Bank RG24: Lych . . .1H 17
Cowslip Way SP11: E Ant . . .2J 37
Crabtree Way RG24: Old Bas . .5K 17
CRANBOURNE 7C 16
Cranbourne Ct.
RG21: B'toke 7C 16
Cranbourne La.
RG21: B'toke 1B 24
Cranesfield RG24: Sher J . . .4A 8
Cranes Rd. RG24: Sher J . . .4K 7
(not continuous)
Crawts Rd. RG25: Over 4C 32
Crescent, The RG24: B'toke . .1K 15
(not continuous)
RG26: B'ley 4B 4
(off The Street)
SP10: A'ver 6B 36
SP11: G Cla 6E 38
SP11: Up C 3D 38
Cress Gdns. SP10: A'ver . . .1E 38
Creswell RG27: Hoo 7D 12
Cricketers Way SP10: A'ver . .3G 37
Cricket Grn. RG27: H Win . . .2K 13
Cricket Grn.
RG27: H Win 2K 13
Cricklade Pl. SP10: A'ver . . .5D 36
Crockford La.
RG24: B'toke, Chin 7F 9
(not continuous)
Croft Av. SP10: A'ver 1F 39
Crofters Mdw. RG24: Lych . . .1H 17
Croft Gdns. SP10: A'ver 1F 39
Crofton Sq. RG27: Sher L . . .3J 9
Croft Rd. RG23: Oak 7A 14
RG27: H Win 4H 13
Crofts, The RG22: B'toke . . .4J 23
Cromwell Cl. RG24: Old Bas . .3K 17
Cromwell Rd. RG21: B'toke . .3C 16
Crondall Ter. RG24: B'toke . .1K 15
Cropmark Way RG22: B'toke . .3H 23
Crossborough Gdns.
RG21: B'toke 5E 16
Crossborough Hill
RG21: B'toke 5E 16
Cross La. SP10: A'ver 6E 36
Cross St. SP10: A'ver 5D 16
Crossways RG28: Whit 5C 30
SP10: A'ver 5E 36
Crown Cres. RG24: Old Bas . .3J 17
Crownfields RG29: Odi 7D 20
Crown Hgts. RG21: B'toke . .4D 16
Crown La. RG24: Old Bas . . .3J 17
RG27: Nat S, Newn 2F 19
Crown Way SP10: A'ver 6J 37
Croye Cl. SP10: A'ver 6E 36
Cuckoo Cl. RG25: Nth W . . .2C 34
(not continuous)
Cuckoo Leaze RG26: Cha A . .1F 7
CUFAUDE 1F 9
RG26: B'ley 6A 4
Cufaude La. RG24: Chin 4H 9
Cuffelle Cl. RG24: Chin 5J 9
Culver Rd. RG21: B'toke . . .6C 16
Cumberland Av.
RG22: B'toke 1A 24
Cummins Cl. SP10: A'ver . . .7H 37
Curlew Cl. RG22: B'toke . . .1G 23
Cusden Dr. SP10: A'ver 4F 37
Cutting Dr. RG24: B'toke . . .1K 15
Cuxhaven Way SP10: A'ver . .3E 36
Cypress Gro. SP10: A'ver . . .7B 36
Cyprus Rd. RG22: B'toke . . .5J 23

D

Dacre Cl. SP10: Charl 3C 36
Daffodil Cl. RG22: B'toke . . .2G 23
Dahlia Cl. RG22: B'toke 2H 23
Dahlia Cl. SP10: A'ver 1C 38
Dairy Wlk. RG27: H Win 2K 13
Dalewood RG22: B'toke 7G 15
Damsel Path RG24: B'toke . .4F 17
Damson Dr. RG27: H Win . . .4J 13
Dancers Mdw. RG24: Sher J . .5B 8
Dances Cl. SP10: A'ver 5G 37
Dance's La. RG28: Whit 5C 30
Danebury Rd. RG22: B'toke . .4H 23
Danegeld Cl. SP10: A'ver . . .2G 37
Danehurst Pl. SP10: A'ver . . .6B 36
Danes, The RG21: B'toke . . .4E 16

DANESHILL 1F 17
Daneshill Ct. RG24: Lych 7H 9
Daneshill Dr. RG24: Lych . . .1H 17
Daneshill E. Ind. Est.
RG24: B'toke 2G 17
Daneshill Ind. Est.
RG24: B'toke 2G 17
Daneshill Rdbt.
RG24: B'toke 2G 17
Daneshill W. Ind. Est.
RG24: B'toke 1F 17
Daniel Rd. RG28: Whit 7D 30
Dankworth Rd. RG22: B'toke . .2J 23
(not continuous)
Darcy Cl. RG21: B'toke 2E 16
D'arcy Ho. RG22: B'toke 7J 15
Darent Cl. RG21: B'toke 4F 17
(off Loddon Dr.)
Dark La. RG24: Sher J 5A 8
Darlington Rd. RG21: B'toke . .2C 16
Dart Ct. SP10: A'ver 4H 37
(off River Way)
Dartmouth Wlk.
RG22: B'toke 6J 15
Dartmouth Way
RG22: B'toke 6J 15
Darwell Ho. RG21: B'toke . . .4C 16
(off Essex Rd.)
Davenport Ga. SP10: A'ver . .5B 36
Davy Cl. RG22: B'toke 5A 16
DEANE 2K 33
Deane Cotts. RG25: Dea 2K 33
Deanes Cl. RG21: B'toke . . .3E 16
Deep La. RG21: B'toke 4B 16
Deerfield Cl. RG26: B'ley 5E 4
Deer Pk. Vw. RG29: Odi 6E 20
Defiance Way SP11: A'ver . . .7K 37
De La Rue Ho.
RG21: B'toke 3F 17
Delibes Rd. RG22: B'toke . . .2B 24
Delius Cl. RG22: B'toke 1A 24
Dell, The RG24: Old Bas 4A 18
Dellands RG25: Over 4C 32
Dellands La. RG25: Over 4B 32
Dellfield RG23: Oak 6B 14
Dell Rd. SP10: A'ver 5E 36
Dene Ct. SP10: A'ver 7G 37
Dene Path SP10: A'ver 7G 37
Dene Rd. SP10: A'ver 7G 37
Denham Dr. RG22: B'toke . . .7J 15
Denning Mead SP10: A'ver . .7E 36
Denvale Trade Pk.
RG21: B'toke 2B 16
De Port Gdns. RG24: Old Bas . .6J 9
Depot, The
Andover 4B 36
Deptford La. RG29: Grey 6K 19
Derbyfields RG29: N War . . .3C 20
Derwent Ct. SP10: A'ver 4H 37
(off Clyde Ct.)
Derwent Rd. RG22: B'toke . . .1G 23
Dever Way RG23: Oak 1B 22
Devizes Cl. RG22: Wort 6G 15
Devonshire Bus. Pk.
RG21: B'toke 2B 16
Devonshire Pl. RG21: B'toke . .5C 16
Dewpond Wlk. RG24: Lych . .1H 17
Dexter Sq. SP10: A'ver 3H 37
Diana Cl. RG22: B'toke 6A 16
Dibley Cl. RG22: B'toke 6J 15
Dicken's La. RG24: Old Bas . .5J 17
RG25: Tun 1H 25
Dilly La. RG27: H Win 4J 13
Dinwoodie Dr. RG24: B'toke . .1A 16
DIPLEY 1E 12
Dipley Rd.
RG27: H Win, Matt 1C 12
Dixon Rd. RG26: B'ley 6D 4
Doctors Acre RG27: Hoo 6D 12
Dollis Grn. RG26: B'ley 4C 4
Dominica Cl. RG22: B'toke . . .6E 8
Domitian Gdns.
RG24: B'toke 1J 15
Don Allen Dr. RG24: Sher J . .7B 8
Dorchester Cl. RG24: B'toke . .4H 15
Dorchester Rd. RG27: Hoo . .7A 12
Dorchester Way
RG29: Grey 5A 20
Dorrel Cl. RG22: B'toke 4H 23
Dorset Cres. RG22: Wort . . .6G 15
Doswell Way RG21: B'toke . .3E 16

Doughty Way SP10: A'ver 5K 37
Douglas Rd. SP11: A'ver 6A 36
Dove Cl. RG22: B'toke 1F 23
  SP10: A'ver 4G 37
Dover Cl. RG23: B'toke 3K 15
Downside Cl. RG24: B'toke 2K 15
Downsland Ct. RG21: B'toke . . .5B 16
  (off Downsland Rd.)
Downsland Pde.
  RG21: B'toke 5B 16
Downsland Rd.
  RG21: B'toke 5B 16
Down St. RG25: Dumm 2H 35
Dragonfly Dr. RG24: Lych 1H 17
Drake Ct. SP10: A'ver 5J 37
Driftway Rd. RG27: Hoo 7C 12
Drive, The RG23: Oak 2B 22
Drove, The SP10: A'ver 6C 36
Dryden Cl. RG24: B'toke 7E 8
Duddon Way RG21: B'toke 4F 17
Dudley Cl. RG23: B'toke 4H 15
Duke Cl. SP10: A'ver 5J 37
DUMMER 2H 35
DUMMER CLUMP 2K 35
Dummer Down La.
  RG25: Dumm 4F 35
Dummer Golf Course 1J 35
Duncan Ct. SP10: A'ver 6J 37
Dundee Gdns. RG22: B'toke . . .5H 15
Dunley's Hill
  RG29: N War, Odi 5C 20
Dunmow Rd. SP10: A'ver 1G 39
Dunsford Cres.
  RG23: B'toke 2J 15
Durham Way RG22: B'toke 2H 23
Durley Cl. SP10: A'ver 7D 36

E

Eagle Cl. RG22: B'toke 2F 23
Eagle Ct. RG24: B'toke 3H 17
Eardley Av. SP10: A'ver 5C 36
EAST ANTON 2H 37
Eastern Av. SP10: A'ver 7G 37
Easter Sq. RG24: B'toke 1K 15
Eastfield Av. RG21: B'toke 4E 16
Eastfield Cl. SP10: A'ver 6H 37
Eastfield Lodge SP10: A'ver . . .6G 37
  (off Eastfield Rd.)
Eastfield Rd. SP10: A'ver 6G 37
EAST OAKLEY 1C 22
East Portway SP10: A'ver 6B 36
EASTROP 5F 17
Eastrop La. RG21: B'toke 4E 16
Eastrop Rdbt. RG21: B'toke 4E 16
Eastrop Way RG21: B'toke 4E 16
East St. SP10: A'ver 6G 37
Edgar Cl. SP10: A'ver 2G 37
Edgehill Cl. RG22: B'toke 6H 15
Edison Gate SP10: A'ver 4A 36
Edison Rd. RG21: B'toke 2A 16
Edmund Ct. RG24: B'toke 7E 8
Edrich Sq. SP10: A'ver 4G 37
Egerton Dr. RG24: B'toke 6D 8
Elbe Way SP10: A'ver 3E 36
Elbow Cnr. RG21: B'toke 4D 16
Elderberry Bank RG24: Lych . . .1H 17
Elder Cres. SP10: A'ver 1C 38
Elder Ho. RG24: Old Bas 4B 18
Elder Rd. RG24: B'toke 1K 15
Elgar Cl. RG22: B'toke 2A 24
Eling Cres. RG27: Sher L 3J 9
Elizabethan Ri.
  RG25: Nth W 1C 34
Elizabeth Rd. RG22: B'toke 6A 16
Ellen Gdns. RG26: B'ley 4B 4
Ellington Cl. SP11: A'ver 7A 36
Ellington Dr. RG22: B'toke 3J 23
Elm Bank Rd. SP10: A'ver 1F 39
Elm Rd. RG24: Sher J 6K 7
  RG25: Over 1D 32
Elms, The SP10: A'ver 7E 36
Elms Rd. RG22: B'toke 6A 12
Elmwood Pde. RG23: B'toke . . .2J 15
Elmwood Way RG23: B'toke . . .2J 15
Elvetham Ri. RG24: Old Bas 7J 9
Emden Rd. SP10: A'ver 3E 36
Englefield Way RG24: B'toke . . .6D 8

English Wood RG24: B'toke 2J 15
Enham Arch Rdbt.
  SP10: A'ver 4G 37
Enham La.
  SP10: Charl, K Enh 3D 36
Ennerdale Cl. RG22: B'toke 7H 15
Enterprise Ct. RG24: B'toke 2F 17
Esher Cl. RG22: B'toke 1K 23
Essex Rd. RG21: B'toke 4C 16
Ethelbert Dr. SP10: Charl 3C 36
Eton Cl. RG22: B'toke 4G 23
Europa Cl. RG26: B'ley 4C 4
Euskirchen Way
  RG22: B'toke 4J 15
Eversfield Cl. SP10: A'ver 6E 36
Evesham Wlk. RG24: B'toke 7D 8
Evingar Gdns. RG28: Whit 5C 30
Evingar Ind. Est.
  RG28: Whit 6C 30
Evingar Rd. RG28: Whit 6C 30
Ewhurst Rd. RG26: Rams 4A 6
Exbury Way SP10: A'ver 7D 36
Exeter Cl. RG22: B'toke 3H 23
Exmoor Cl. RG22: B'toke 6H 15
Eynsham Wlk. RG24: B'toke 7C 8

F

Fabian Cl. RG21: B'toke 5C 16
Fairclose RG28: Whit 7B 30
  (not continuous)
Fairclose Ter. RG28: Whit 6C 30
  (off Fairclose)
Fairfield RG28: Whit 5C 30
Fairfields Arts Cen. 5D 16
Fairfields Rd. RG21: B'toke 6D 16
Fairholme Pde. RG27: Hoo 7A 12
FAIR OAK GREEN 1E 4
Fair Oak La. RG7: Stra S 1E 4
Fairthorne Ho. RG22: B'toke 1E 16
Fairthorne Ri.
  RG24: Old Bas 4A 18
Fairview Mdw. RG23: Oak 2B 22
Falcon Cl. RG22: B'toke 1F 23
Falkland Rd. RG24: B'toke 6E 8
Fanum Ho. RG21: B'toke 3F 17
Faraday Cl. RG24: B'toke 1F 17
Faraday Office Pk.
  RG24: B'toke 1F 17
Faraday Pk. SP10: A'ver 5A 36
Faraday Rd. RG24: B'toke 1F 17
Faringdon Ct. RG24: B'toke 7C 8
Farleigh La.
  RG25: Dumm, Far W
    . . . . .2H 35 & 7H 23
Farleigh Ri. RG21: B'toke 7E 16
Farleigh Rd.
  RG25: Clid, Far W 7K 23
FARLEIGH WALLOP 7A 24
Farm Cotts. RG24: B'toke 1K 15
Farm Ground Cl. RG27: Hoo 7C 12
Farm Rd. SP11: A'ver 1A 38
Farm Vw. Dr. RG24: Chin 5J 9
Farnham Rd. RG29: Odi 6E 20
Faroe Cl. RG24: B'toke 7F 9
Farriers Cl. RG26: B'ley 4C 4
Farrs Av. SP10: A'ver 1G 39
Fayrewood Chase
  RG21: B'toke 3H 23
Feathers La. RG21: B'toke 5D 16
Feathers Yd. RG21: B'toke 5D 16
Felders Mede RG27: Hoo 7D 12
Feld Way RG24: Lych 1J 17
Fencott Pl. RG21: B'toke 3D 16
Fennel Cl. RG24: Chin 4J 9
Ferguson Cl. RG21: B'toke 7D 16
Ferndale Gdns. RG27: Hoo 6A 12
Ferndale Rd. SP10: A'ver 5D 36
Ferndown Cl. RG22: B'toke 6G 23
Fernhill Pl. RG27: Sher L 3K 9
Ferrell Fld. RG27: Hoo 7K 11
Festival Pl. RG21: B'toke 4D 16
Fieldways RG21: B'toke 6E 16
Fiji Cl. RG24: B'toke 7F 9
Fingle Dr. SP10: A'ver 6D 36
Finkley Down Farm Pk. 3K 37
Finkley Rd. SP11: Sman 2J 37
Firecrest Rd. RG22: B'toke 3F 23
Firs, The SP10: A'ver 6D 36
Firs La. RG29: Odi 7C 20

Firs Way RG23: B'toke 2H 15
Firsway RG28: Whit 6C 30
  (not continuous)
Fisher Cl. RG24: B'toke 7C 8
  SP10: A'ver 6J 37
Fiske Cl. RG22: B'toke 5J 15
Fitness First
  Chineham 4G 9
FLAT FIRS 5H 7
Flaxfield Ct. RG21: B'toke 4C 16
Flaxfield Rd. RG21: B'toke 4C 16
Fleet Rd.
  RG27: H Win, Winchf 2K 13
Flensburg Cl. SP10: A'ver 3E 36
Fletcher Cl. RG21: B'toke 5B 16
Flinders Cl. SP10: A'ver 5K 37
Flint Cl. SP10: A'ver 1D 38
Floral Way SP10: A'ver 1C 38
Florence Ct. SP10: A'ver 3G 37
  (not continuous)
Florence Portal Cl.
  RG28: L'stoke 6J 31
Florence Way RG24: B'toke 1J 15
Flowerdew Ct. RG21: B'toke 1G 39
Focus 303 Bus. Cen.
  SP10: A'ver 5J 37
Focus Way SP10: A'ver 5J 37
Folly La. RG7: Stra S 4E 4
  RG26: B'ley 4E 4
Folly Roundabout, The
  SP10: A'ver 5E 36
Ford La. RG25: Up G 3K 27
Forde Rd. RG29: S War 3K 27
Forest Dr. RG24: Chin 4H 9
Forfield Dr. RG22: B'toke 5G 23
Forge Cl. RG26: B'ley 5D 4
Forge Fld. SP10: A'ver 5G 37
Forsythia Wlk.
  RG21: B'toke 1E 16
Forth Cl. SP10: A'ver 4H 37
Fort Hill Dr. RG23: B'toke 3J 15
Forum Cl. RG23: B'toke 4H 15
Fosters Bus. Pk.
  RG27: Hoo 1J 19
Foundry Cl. RG27: Hoo 7A 12
Foundry Rd. SP11: An V 3B 38
Fountains Cl. RG24: B'toke 7C 8
Fountain's Mall RG29: Odi 6E 20
Four Acre Coppice
  RG24: B'toke 6C 12
Four Lanes Cl. RG24: Chin 5J 9
FOXCOTTE 3B 36
Foxcotte Cl. SP10: Charl 4C 36
Foxcotte La. SP10: Charl 3B 36
  SP11: Charl 3B 36
Foxcotte Rd. SP10: Charl 3A 36
  SP11: Pen M 3A 36
FOXDOWN 1D 32
Foxdown RG25: Over 1D 32
Foxglove Cl. RG22: B'toke 3G 23
FOXHALL 7J 23
Fox La. RG23: Oak 6C 14
Foxmoor Cl. RG23: Oak 6B 14
Fox's Furlong RG24: Chin 4K 9
Foyle Pl. RG21: B'toke 7C 16
Frances Rd. RG21: B'toke 5C 16
Franklin Av. RG27: H Win 1J 13
Fraser Cl. RG24: Old Bas 3K 17
FREEFOLK 5G 31
Freefolk Priors RG28: Free 5G 31
Freemantle Cl. RG21: B'toke . . .2F 17
Frescade Cres.
  RG21: B'toke 6C 16
Frithmead Cl. RG21: B'toke 7C 16
Frog La. RG25: Mapl 4D 18
  RG27: Roth 1H 11
Frome Cl. RG21: B'toke 4F 17
  RG23: Oak 1C 22
Froome Pl. RG24: Chin 6G 9
Frouds Cl. RG27: Hoo 1K 19
Froyle La.
  RG29: L Sut, S War 7A 28
Fry Sq. SP10: A'ver 4G 37
  (off Cricketers Way)
Fulbrook Way RG29: Odi 2D 28
Fulham Rd. RG21: B'toke 4D 16
  (off Festival Pl.)
Fullerton Rd.
  SP11: G Cla, Red R 6A 38
Fulmar Cl. RG22: B'toke 3F 23
Furrow Way SP11: E Ant 2H 37

Fuzzy Drove RG22: B'toke . . . . . .2. . .
Fylingdales Cl.
  RG22: B'toke . . . . .5. . .

G

Gage Cl. RG24: Lych . . . . .2. . .
Gaiger Av. RG27: Sher L . . . .
Gainsborough Ct.
  SP10: A'ver . . . . .5. . .
Gainsborough Rd.
  RG21: B'toke . . . . .7. . .
Gala Bingo
  Basingstoke . . . . .4. . .
Galahad Cl. SP10: A'ver . . . . . . .4. . .
Gales Ct. SP10: A'ver . . . . .6. . .
Galileo Pk. SP10: A'ver . . . . .6. . .
Gallaghers Mead
  SP10: A'ver . . . . .6. . .
Galloway Cl. RG22: B'toke . . . . . .6. . .
Gander Dr. RG24: B'toke . . . . . . .1. . .
Gannet Cl. RG22: B'toke . . . . . . .5. . .
Garden Cl. RG27: Hoo . . . . .7. . .
  SP10: A'ver . . . . .7. . .
Gardiner Rd. RG24: B'toke . . . . . .4. . .
Garrett Ct. RG23: Oak . . . . .1. . .
Garside Cl. RG26: B'ley . . . .
Gaston La. RG29: S War . . . . . . .3. . .
Gastons Wood RG24: Chin . . . . . .
Gateswood Dr. RG27: Sher L . . . .
Gawaine Cl. SP10: A'ver . . . . . . .2. . .
Geffery's Flds. RG21: B'toke . . . .5. . .
Geffery's Ho. RG27: Hoo . . . . . . .6. . .
Genoa Ct. SP10: A'ver . . . . .2C. . .
  (not continu. . .
George St. RG21: B'toke . . . . . . .4. . .
George Yd. SP10: A'ver . . . . .7. . .
Georgia Cl. SP10: A'ver . . . . . . .7. . .
German Rd. RG26: B'ley . . . .
Gershwin Cl. RG22: B'toke . . . . . .2. . .
Gershwin Rd. RG22: B'toke . . . . .2. . .
Gibbons Pl. RG24: B'toke . . . . . .
Gilbard Cl. RG24: Chin . . . .
Gilbert Cl. RG24: B'toke . . . .
Gilberts Mead Cl.
  SP11: An V . . . . .3. . .
Gillies Dr. RG24: B'toke . . . . . . .1. . .
Glade Cl. RG24: Chin . . . .
Glamis Cl. RG23: Oak . . . . .7. . .
Glastonbury Cl.
  RG24: B'toke . . . . .1. . .
Glebe Cl. RG25: Dumm . . . . .2. . .
Glebe Ho. RG21: B'toke . . . . . . .3. . .
  (off Vyne. . .
Glebelands SP11: G Cla . . . . . . .6. . .
Glebe La. RG23: Wort . . . . .5. . .
  RG27: H Win . . . . .3. . .
Glebe Mdw. RG25: Over . . . . . . .3. . .
Glen Cl. SP10: A'ver . . . . .6. . .
Gleneagles Cl. RG22: B'toke . . . .6. . .
Glenmore Bus. Pk.
  SP10: A'ver . . . . .7. . .
Gloucester Dr. RG22: B'toke . . . .2. . .
Goat La. RG21: B'toke . . . . .4. . .
Goch Way SP10: A'ver, Charl . . . .4. . .
Goddards Cl. RG27: Sher L . . . . .
Goddards Firs RG23: Oak . . . . . .2. . .
Goddards La. RG27: Sher L . . . . .
Goddards Mead SP10: A'ver . . . .7. . .
Goddard Sq. SP10: A'ver . . . .
  (off Cricketers. . .
Golden Lion Rdbt.
  RG21: B'toke . . . . .7. . .
Goldfinch Gdns.
  RG22: B'toke . . . . .4. . .
Goodchilds Hill RG7: Stra S . . . . .
Goodman Cl. RG21: B'toke . . . . .5. . .
GOODWORTH CLATFORD . . . . . .5. . .
Goodworth Vw. SP11: G Cla . . . .6. . .
Goose Grn. RG27: Hoo . . . . .6. . .
Goose La. RG27: Hoo . . . . .6. . .
Gordon Brown Outdoor Education
  Centre, The . . . . .6. . .
Gordon Cl. RG21: B'toke . . . . . . .3. . .
Gower Cl. RG21: B'toke . . . . .2. . .
Gower Cres. RG27: Hoo . . . . . . .7. . .
Gracemere Cres.
  RG22: B'toke . . . . .3. . .
Grace Sq. SP10: A'ver . . . . .4. . .
Grafton Way RG22: B'toke . . . . .5. . .

...ger Cl. RG22: B'toke 1A **24**
...Wlk. SP11: E Ant 2H **37**
...pian Way RG22: B'toke ..6H **15**
...ada Pl. SP10: A'ver 5H **37**
...d Pde. RG27: Hoo 7A **12**
...ge La. RG27: H Win 2H **13**
...eney Sq. SP10: A'ver 4G **37**
(off Cricketers Way)
...infields Cres.
RG24: Lych 1H **17**
...infields Rd.
RG24: Chin, Lych 7H **9**
...t Marlow RG27: Hoo 7D **12**
...t Oaks Chase
RG24: Chin 6G **9**
...heldons Coppice
RG27: Hoo 7K **11**
...Western Cotts.
...e Cl. RG22: B'toke 3D **16**
...n, The RG25: Over 3D **32**
RG28: Whit 6D **30**
RG29: N War 4B **20**
SP10: Charl 3D **36**
SP11: Up C 3D **38**
...naways, The
RG23: Oak 7B **14**
...nbirch Cl. RG22: B'toke ..3F **23**
...nbury Cl. RG23: B'toke ...4J **15**
...nhaven Cl. SP10: A'ver ..7H **37**
...nlands Rd.
RG24: B'toke 1K **15**
...n La. RG27: H Win 3J **13**
RG27: Roth 4J **11**
...en La. Gdns.
RG27: H Win 4J **13**
...enly Ct. SP10: A'ver 7E **36**
...en Mdw. La. SP11: G Cla ..5F **39**
...n Way RG22: B'toke 4J **15**
RG23: B'toke 3J **15**
...enway RG27: Sher L 7G **5**
...enwich Way SP10: A'ver ..4F **37**
...enwood Dr. RG24: Chin ...4H **9**
...enwoods RG28: Whit 5C **30**
...ory Cl. RG21: B'toke 2E **16**
...ory Ho. RG27: Hoo 7A **12**
...sley Rd. RG21: B'toke ...3E **16**
RG24: B'toke 3E **16**
...hound La. RG25: Over ...4C **32**
...YWELL 6K **19**
...vwell Rd.
RG24: Mapl, Old Bas ...4B **18**
RG25: Mapl 4B **18**
RG27: A'ell, Up N 4F **19**
...g Cl. RG24: B'toke 1A **24**
...in Way Nth. RG27: Hoo ..5B **12**
...in Way Sth. RG27: Hoo ..6C **12**
...svenor Cl. RG22: B'toke ..5H **23**
...svenor Ho. RG22: B'toke ..4E **16**
...ve Cl. RG21: B'toke 6E **16**
...ve Ho. RG24: Lych 7H **9**
...ve Rd. RG21: B'toke 7D **16**
...ves Orchard RG28: Whit ..6B **30**
...enea Ct. RG24: B'toke ...6E **8**
...rsey Cl. RG24: Chin 4J **9**
...ney Ct. RG29: Odi 7D **20**

H

...kwood Cl. SP10: A'ver ...7C **36**
...kwood Cotts.
RG21: B'toke 7E **16**
...kwood La. RG25: Clid 4C **24**
...kwood Rd. RG21: B'toke ..5D **16**
...kwood Rd. Rdbt.
RG21: B'toke 6E **16**
...rian Rd. SP10: A'ver 3G **37**
...rians Way RG23: B'toke ..2J **15**
...ra Pl. SP10: A'ver 6D **36**
...stone Rd. RG21: B'toke ..1D **16**
...fax Cl. SP10: A'ver 5E **36**
...iday Cl. RG21: B'toke ...7C **16**
...s La. RG27: Matt 1J **11**
...leigh Pl. RG21: B'toke ...1J **17**
...ble Cl. RG23: Oak 1B **22**
...ble Ct. RG21: B'toke 4F **17**
SP10: A'ver 4H **37**
...bledon Way
RG27: Sher L 3K **9**
...burg Cl. SP10: A'ver 3E **36**

Hamelyn Cl. RG21: B'toke ..5C **16**
Hamelyn Rd. RG21: B'toke ..5C **16**
Hamilton Cl. RG21: B'toke ..1K **13**
Hammond Rd. RG21: B'toke ..6C **16**
Hammond Sq. *SP10: A'ver* ..4G **37**
(off Cricketers Way)
HAMPSHIRE BMI CLINIC ...3G **17**
Hampshire Cl. RG22: Wort ..6G **15**
Hampshire Golf Course, The
..........5G **39**
Hampshire Intl. Bus. Pk.
RG24: Chin 4G **9**
Hampstead Ho.
RG21: B'toke 4D **16**
(off Festival Pl.)
Hampton Ct. RG23: B'toke ..3K **15**
Hams Cnr. RG27: Sher L 1C **10**
Handel Cl. RG22: B'toke 1A **24**
Hanmore Rd. RG24: Chin ...6G **9**
Hanover Cl. SP10: A'ver 1C **38**
Hanover Gdns. RG21: B'toke ..7C **16**
Hanover Ho. *SP10: A'ver* ...7G **37**
(off Kings Mdw.)
Hanson Rd. SP10: A'ver 5D **36**
Hardings La. RG27: H Win ..2K **13**
Hardy La. RG21: B'toke 5C **16**
Harebell Cl. RG27: H Win ...1K **13**
Harebell Gdns.
RG27: H Win 1K **13**
Hare's La. RG27: H Win 1K **13**
Harewood Mobile Home Pk.
SP11: And D 5K **37**
Harfield Cl. RG27: Hoo 7A **12**
Hargreaves Cl. RG24: B'toke ..7E **8**
Harlech Cl. RG23: B'toke ...4J **15**
Harness Ct. RG24: B'toke ...1K **15**
Harold Jackson Ter.
SP11: B'toke 5E **16**
Harris Hill RG22: B'toke ...3H **23**
Harrison Pl. RG21: B'toke ..4C **16**
Harroway RG28: Hur P, Whit ..3A **30**
Harrow Way
RG22: B'toke 1A **24**
SP10: A'ver 5A **36**
Hartford Ct. RG27: H Win ..2J **13**
Hartford Rd. RG27: H Win ..2J **13**
Hartford Ter. RG27: H Win ..2K **13**
Hart Ho. Ct. RG27: H Win ..2K **13**
Hartley La. RG27: H Wes ...5J **5**
Hartley Mdw. RG28: Whit ...6B **30**
Hartley M. RG27: H Win 1K **13**
HARTLEY WESPALL 1F **11**
HARTLEY WINTNEY 2K **13**
Hartley Wintney Golf Course
..........1K **13**
Hartswood RG24: Chin 6G **9**
Harvest Way RG24: Lych 2H **17**
Harvey Pl. SP10: A'ver 6J **37**
Harvey's Fld. RG25: Over ...3C **32**
Hassocks Workshops
RG24: B'toke 2G **17**
Hastings Cl. RG23: B'toke ..4H **15**
HATCH 4B **18**
Hatch La. RG24: Old Bas ...3K **17**
Hatch Pk. (Caravan Pk.)
RG24: Old Bas 4A **18**
HATCH WARREN 3H **23**
Hatch Warren Cotts.
RG22: B'toke 3J **23**
Hatchwarren Gdns.
RG22: B'toke 3A **24**
Hatch Warren La.
RG22: B'toke 3H **23**
Hatch Warren Retail Pk.
RG22: B'toke 4G **23**
Hatch Warren Way
RG22: B'toke 3A **24**
Hathaway Gdns.
RG24: B'toke 1F **17**
Hatherden Ct. *SP10: A'ver* ..6G **37**
(off Eastfield Rd.)
Hattem Pl. SP10: A'ver 3E **36**
Hawk Cl. RG22: B'toke 2F **23**
Hawke Cl. SP10: A'ver 5J **37**
Hawkes Cl. RG27: H Win ...1J **13**
Hawkfield La. RG21: B'toke ..5C **16**
Hawthorn Ri. RG27: Hoo ...6B **12**
Hawthorn Way
RG23: B'toke 3J **15**
Haydn Rd. RG22: B'toke ...2K **23**
Hayle Cl. RG23: Oak 4H **15**

Hayley La. RG29: L Sut 5B **28**
Haymarket Theatre 5D **16**
Haywarden Pl. RG27: H Win ..1K **13**
Hazel Cl. RG23: Oak 1B **22**
SP10: A'ver 1C **38**
Hazelcombe RG25: Over 4D **32**
Hazel Coppice RG27: Hoo ...6B **12**
Hazeldene RG24: Chin 6H **9**
Hazeley Cl. RG27: H Win ...4J **13**
Hazeli Cl. RG27: H Win 4J **13**
Hazelwood RG24: Chin 4G **9**
Hazelwood Cl. RG23: B'toke ..2K **15**
Hazelwood Dr.
RG23: B'toke 2K **15**
Headington Cl. RG22: B'toke ..2K **23**
Heather Dr. SP10: A'ver 5E **36**
Heather Gro. RG27: H Win ..1J **13**
Heather La. RG27: Up N ...4G **19**
HEATHER ROW 3J **19**
Heather Row La.
RG27: Nat S, Up N 2J **19**
Heather Way RG22: B'toke ..3G **23**
Heathfield RG22: B'toke 3K **23**
Heathside Way RG27: H Win ..1J **13**
Heath Va. SP10: A'ver 7G **37**
Heathview RG27: Hoo 6C **12**
Hedge End Pl. SP10: A'ver ..1G **39**
Hedgerows, The
RG21: B'toke 1J **17**
Hedgerow Way SP11: E Ant ..3H **37**
Hedges Footpath
SP10: A'ver 7E **36**
Hele Cl. RG21: B'toke 7C **16**
Helford Ct. SP10: A'ver 4H **37**
Hendren Sq. SP10: A'ver ...4H **37**
Hengest Cl. SP10: Charl 3C **36**
Hepplewhite Dr.
RG22: B'toke 3G **23**
Hepworth Cl. SP10: A'ver ...5F **37**
Herdwick Rd. SP11: E Ant ..2J **37**
Hereford Cl. RG29: Odi 7C **20**
Hereford Rd. RG23: B'toke ..4J **15**
Heritage Pk. RG22: B'toke ..5H **23**
Heritage Vw. RG22: B'toke ..5H **23**
Heron Pk. RG24: Lych 7H **9**
Herons Ri. SP10: A'ver 1G **39**
Heronswood RG29: Odi 5F **21**
Heron Way RG22: B'toke ...2F **23**
Herriard Pl. RG22: B'toke ..5G **23**
Herridge Cl. RG26: B'ley ...5E **4**
Hewitt Rd. RG24: B'toke ...6D **8**
Hexagon, The SP10: A'ver ..1C **38**
Hibiscus Cres. SP10: A'ver ..7B **36**
Hides Cl. RG28: Whit 7C **30**
High Beech Gdns.
SP10: A'ver 7H **37**
Highbury Rd. SP11: An V ...3C **38**
Highdowns RG22: B'toke ...4J **23**
High Dr. RG22: B'toke 7J **15**
Higher Mead RG24: Lych ...1H **17**
Highfield Chase
RG21: B'toke 4B **16**
Highfields RG25: Over 4D **32**
Highland Dr. RG23: Oak ...7A **14**
Highlands Rd. RG22: Wort ..6G **15**
Highmoors RG24: Chin 5H **9**
Highpath Ct. RG24: B'toke ..2K **15**
Highpath M. RG24: B'toke ..2K **15**
Highpath Way RG24: B'toke ..1J **15**
High St. RG25: Over 3C **32**
RG27: H Win 2K **13**
RG29: Odi 6D **20**
SP10: A'ver 7F **37**
Highview Bus. Pk.
RG27: Hoo 1H **19**
Highwood Ridge
RG22: B'toke 4H **23**
Hillary Rd. RG21: B'toke ...2B **16**
Hillbury Av. SP10: A'ver ...1D **38**
Hillcrest Cl. RG23: B'toke ..3H **15**
Hillcrest Wlk. RG23: B'toke ..4H **15**
Hill Meadow RG25: Over ...1C **32**
Hill Rd. RG23: Oak 1A **22**
HILL SIDE 7H **21**
Hillside Cl. RG28: Whit 6E **30**
Hillside Ct. SP10: A'ver 7E **36**
Hillside Rd. RG28: Over 1E **28**
Hillside Vs. SP10: Charl 4D **36**
Hill Sq. RG24: Lych 7J **9**
Hillstead Ct. RG21: B'toke ..5E **16**

Hills Way RG26: B'ley 5C **4**
Hilltop Rd. RG25: Over 1D **32**
Hill Vw. Rd. RG22: B'toke ..6A **16**
Hines Ct. RG24: B'toke 1K **15**
Hobbs Cl. RG24: B'toke 7K **7**
Hobbs Sq. *SP10: A'ver* 4H **37**
(off Cricketers Way)
Hockney Grn. SP10: A'ver ..5F **37**
HODDINGTON 5F **27**
Hogarth Cl. RG21: B'toke ..5G **17**
Hogarth Ct. SP10: A'ver ...4E **36**
Holbein Cl. RG21: B'toke ...6F **17**
Holland Dr. SP10: A'ver 3E **36**
Hollies, The RG24: Old Bas ..4B **18**
RG27: H Win 4J **13**
Hollies Ct. RG24: B'toke ...1K **15**
Hollies Ind. Estate, The
RG24: Old Bas 4B **18**
Hollin's Wlk. *RG21: B'toke* ..4D **16**
(off Festival Pl.)
Holly Cl. RG26: B'ley 5D **4**
HOLLY CROSS 2D **4**
Holly Dr. RG24: Old Bas ...3A **18**
Hollyhock Cl. RG22: B'toke ..2G **23**
Holly Ho. RG24: Old Bas ...4B **18**
Holly Wlk. RG27: Hoo 1C **38**
Holman Cl. RG26: B'ley 5E **4**
Holmes Cl. RG22: B'toke ...4J **23**
Holmes Cl. SP10: A'ver 7D **36**
Holst Cl. RG22: B'toke 3A **24**
Holt La. RG27: Hoo 2C **20**
Holt Way RG27: Hoo 6C **12**
Holy Barn Cl. RG22: B'toke ..6H **15**
Holyrood Cl. RG22: B'toke ..6H **15**
Home Farm Gdns.
SP10: Charl 3C **36**
Homefield Way RG24: B'toke ..7J **7**
Home Mead RG25: Nth W ..2D **34**
Homesteads Rd.
RG22: B'toke 1G **23**
Honeyleaze RG22: B'toke ...5G **23**
Honeysuckle Cl.
RG22: B'toke 2G **23**
Honeysuckle Gdns.
SP10: A'ver 7B **36**
Hood Cl. SP10: A'ver 6J **37**
HOOK 7A **12**
HOOK COMMON 2K **19**
Hook La. RG23: Oak 2A **14**
RG26: Up Woott 2A **14**
Hook Rd. RG27: Roth 2A **20**
RG27: Roth 3K **11**
RG29: Grey, N War 5K **19**
RG29: N War 4C **20**
Hook Station (Rail) 1B **20**
Hoopersmead RG25: Clid ...3C **24**
Hoopers Way RG23: Oak ...1B **22**
Hopfield Rd. RG27: H Win ..3J **13**
Hop Garden Rd. RG27: Hoo ..7K **11**
Hopkinson Way SP10: A'ver ..5A **36**
Hopton Gth. RG24: Lych ...7J **9**
Hornbeam Pl. RG27: Hoo ...6B **12**
Horwood Gdns.
RG21: B'toke 1G **23**
Houghton Sq. RG27: Sher L ..3K **9**
HOUNDMILLS 3A **16**
Houndmills Rd.
RG21: B'toke 3A **16**
Houndmills Rdbt.
RG21: B'toke 2B **16**
Hoursome Ct. RG22: B'toke ..6H **23**
Howard Rd. RG21: B'toke ..6E **16**
Howard Vw. RG22: B'toke ..6K **15**
Hubbard Rd. RG21: B'toke ..2B **16**
Huish La. RG24: Old Bas ...5K **17**
RG25: Tun 5K **17**
Hulbert Way RG22: B'toke ..7J **15**
Humber Ct. *SP10: A'ver* ...4H **37**
(off Itchen Ct.)
Humberstone Rd.
SP10: A'ver 1F **39**
Humming Bird Ct.
RG22: B'toke 2F **23**
(off Heron Way)
Hundred Acre Rdbt.
SP10: A'ver 6B **36**
Hungerford Cl. RG22: Wort ..5G **15**
Hungerford La.
SP10: K Enh 1F **37**
Hunters Cl. RG23: Oak 6B **14**
Hunting Ga. RG21: B'toke ..3A **16**

Hunts Cl. RG27: Hoo 7C 12
Hunts Comn. RG27: H Win 1K 13
Hunts Cotts. RG27: H Win 1K 13
Hurne Ct. RG21: B'toke 4F 17
　　　　　　　　　　(off Lytton Rd.)
Hutchins Way RG24: B'toke 6D 8
Hutton Sq. SP10: A'ver 4H 37
Hyacinth Cl. RG22: B'toke 2G 23
Hyde Rd. RG29: L Sut 7E 28

I

IBWORTH 6A 6
Icknield Ho. SP10: A'ver 4H 37
Icknield Wlk. SP11: E Ant 2H 37
　　　　　　　　(off Augusta Way West)
Icknield Way SP10: A'ver 1G 37
Idsworth Ct. RG24: B'toke 1K 15
Illingworth Cl. RG26: B'ley 5E 4
　　　　　　　　　　(off St Mary's Av.)
Ilsley Rd. RG24: B'toke 6D 8
Imperial Ct. SP10: A'ver 5K 37
Inglewood Dr. RG22: B'toke 4E 22
Inkpen Gdns. RG24: Lych 1J 17
Intec Bus. Cen.
　　RG24: B'toke 1G 17
IO Centre, The RG21: B'toke . .3A 16
Iris Cl. RG22: B'toke 3G 23
Irvine Cres. RG24: B'toke 7E 8
Irwell Cl. RG21: B'toke 4F 17
Itchen Cl. RG23: Oak 1B 22
Itchen Ct. SP10: A'ver 4H 37
Ivar Gdns. RG24: Lych 7J 9

J

Jackdaw Cl. RG22: B'toke 2F 23
Jacob's All. RG21: B'toke 5D 16
Jacobs Cl. SP11: E Ant 2J 37
Jacob's Yd. RG21: B'toke 5D 16
Jameson Ho. RG24: Lych 7H 9
Jardine Sq. SP10: A'ver 4H 37
　　　　　　　　　(off Cricketers Way)
Jasmine Ct. SP10: A'ver 1D 38
　　　　　　　　　　(off Floral Way)
Jasmine Rd. RG22: B'toke 2H 23
Jays Cl. RG22: B'toke 1C 24
Jefferson Rd. RG21: B'toke 2D 16
Jellicoe Ct. SP10: A'ver 5J 37
　　　　　　　　(off Admirals Way)
Jenson Gdns. SP10: A'ver 7D 36
Jersey Cl. RG24: B'toke 6E 8
Jervis Ct. SP10: A'ver 5J 37
Jibbs Mdw. RG26: B'ley 4C 4
Jobson Cl. RG28: Whit 6C 30
John Eddie Ct. RG22: B'toke . .6J 15
John Hunt Dr. RG24: B'toke 7D 8
John Morgan Cl.
　　RG27: Hoo 6A 12
Joices Yd. RG21: B'toke 5D 16
Joule Rd. RG21: B'toke 2B 16
　　SP10: A'ver 5A 36
Jubilee Rd. RG21: B'toke 5D 16
Julius Ct. RG24: B'toke 1J 15
Junction Rd. SP10: A'ver 5E 36
June Dr. RG23: B'toke 4H 15
Juniper Cl. RG24: Chin 4J 9
　　SP10: A'ver 7C 36
Jutland Cres. SP10: A'ver 3E 36

K

Katherine Cl. RG22: B'toke 7G 15
Kathleen Cl. RG21: B'toke 7C 16
Keats Cl. RG24: B'toke 7E 8
Kellys Wlk. SP10: A'ver 7D 36
Kelvin Hill RG22: B'toke 6A 16
Kembers La. RG25: Mapl 5C 18
Kemmitt Way SP10: A'ver 1D 38
KEMPSHOTT 1G 23
Kempshott Gdns.
　　RG22: B'toke 2F 23
Kempshott Gro. RG22: Wort . . .5G 15
Kempshott La. RG22: B'toke . . .3G 23
Kempshott Pk. Ind. Est.
　　RG23: B'toke 7F 23
Kempshott Rdbt.
　　RG22: B'toke 3H 23

Kemys Gdns. SP10: A'ver 6E 36
Kendal Gdns. RG22: B'toke . . .7H 15
Kenilworth Rd.
　　RG23: B'toke 3H 15
Kennet Cl. RG21: B'toke 4F 17
Kennet Ct. SP10: A'ver 4H 37
Kennet Way RG23: Oak 1B 22
Kensington Ho.
　　RG21: B'toke 4D 16
　　　　　　　　　　(off Festival Pl.)
Kenyons Yd. RG21: B'toke 6D 36
Kerchers Fld. RG25: Over 4C 32
Kerfield Way RG27: Hoo 7B 12
Kersley Cres. RG29: Odi 2C 28
Kestrel Rd. RG22: B'toke 1F 23
Ketelbey Ri. RG22: B'toke 3B 24
Kew Cl. RG24: B'toke 6D 8
Kew Wlk. SP10: A'ver 7D 36
Keytech Cen.
　　RG21: B'toke 2K 15
Kidlington Rd. RG24: B'toke . . .7C 8
Kiel Dr. SP10: A'ver 3E 36
Kiln Gdns. RG27: H Win 2J 13
Kiln La. RG26: M She 3G 7
Kiln Rd. RG24: Sher J 5A 8
Kimball Rd. RG21: B'toke 7B 16
Kimber Cl. RG24: Chin 6H 9
Kimberley Cl. SP10: Charl 4D 36
Kimberley Rd.
　　RG22: B'toke 6A 16
Kindersley Pk. Homes
　　SP11: Abb A 4A 38
King Arthur's Way
　　SP10: A'ver 3F 37
King Arthur's Way Rdbt.
　　SP10: A'ver 2G 37
Kingfisher Cl. RG22: B'toke . . .1F 23
　　RG28: Whit 6C 30
Kingfisher Ct. RG21: B'toke . . .3C 16
King George Rd.
　　SP10: A'ver 6C 36
King Johns Rd.
　　RG29: N War 5C 20
Kingsbridge Copse
　　RG27: Newn 1J 19
Kingsbridge End RG27: Hoo . . .1J 19
　　　　　　　　　(off Old School Rd.)
Kings Chase SP10: A'ver 7D 36
Kingsclere Rd.
　　RG21: B'toke 2B 16
　　RG23: W Law 4A 6
　　RG25: Over 1C 32
　　RG26: Rams, Up Woott 4A 6
　　RG28: Whit 3D 30
Kingsland Bus. Pk.
　　RG24: Old Bas 7G 9
Kingsley Pk. RG28: Whit 5C 30
Kingsmead SP11: An V 3B 38
Kings Mdw. RG25: Over 3C 32
Kingsmill Rd.
　　SP10: A'ver 3G 37
Kingsmill Rd.
　　RG21: B'toke 7C 16
Kings Orchard RG23: Oak 2B 22
Kings Pightle RG24: Chin 5H 9
King's Rd. RG22: B'toke 6A 16
Kingston Cl. SP10: A'ver 1D 38
King St. RG29: Odi 6E 20
　　　　　　　　　　　(not continuous)
Kingsvale Ct. RG21: B'toke 5B 16
Kings Wlk. RG28: Whit 6C 30
Kingsway SP10: A'ver 4K 37
Kingsway Gdns.
　　SP10: A'ver 3F 37
Kings Yd. SP10: A'ver 6G 37
Kintyre Cl. RG23: Oak 7A 14
Kipling Wlk. RG22: B'toke 6A 16
Kirby Dr. RG26: B'ley 5C 4
Kite Hill Cotts. RG22: Wort 6G 15
KNIGHTS ENHAM 1F 37
Knights Enham Rdbt.
　　SP10: A'ver 2F 37
Knights Pk. Rd.
　　RG21: B'toke 3B 16
Knight St. RG21: B'toke 5B 16

Knowle Rd. RG24: B'toke 1J 15
Knowlings, The RG28: Whit . . .7D 30

L

Laburnum Way RG23: B'toke . .3K 15
Ladies Wlk. SP10: A'ver 1H 39
Laffans Rd. RG29: Odi 1D 28
Lakeside Cl. SP10: Charl 4C 36
Lake Vw. RG27: H Win 1K 13
Laker Sq. SP10: A'ver 4H 37
Lamb Roundabout, The
　　SP10: A'ver 7G 37
Lambs Cl. RG25: Over 3D 32
Lambs Row RG24: Lych 2H 17
Lampards Cl. RG27: Roth 2K 11
Lampool Ho. RG25: Over 3D 32
　　　　　　　　　　(off Station Rd.)
Lancaster Cl. SP10: A'ver 5E 36
Lancaster Rd. RG21: A'ver 3C 16
Landseer Cl. RG21: B'toke 6F 17
Landseer Ct. SP10: A'ver 5E 36
LANE END 7G 29
Lane End RG26: B'ley 5C 4
Lane's End RG24: Chin 6J 9
Langham Ct. RG27: Sher L 3K 9
Langley Gro. RG27: Sher L 3J 9
Lansdowne Av. SP10: A'ver 1D 38
Lansley Rd. RG21: B'toke 1D 16
Lapin La. RG22: B'toke 5H 23
Lapwing Cl. RG22: B'toke 3F 23
Lapwing Ri. RG28: Whit 6B 30
Larch Dr. SP10: A'ver 7B 36
Larchwood RG24: Chin 5H 9
Lark Cl. RG22: B'toke 2F 23
　　SP10: A'ver 4G 37
Larkfield RG24: Chin 6H 9
Larks Barrow Hill
　　RG28: Whit 1C 30
Larkspur Gdns.
　　RG21: B'toke 6B 16
Larwood Sq. SP10: A'ver 4H 37
　　　　　　　　　(off Cricketers Way)
Launcelot Cl. SP10: A'ver 3F 37
Laundry Yd. RG28: Whit 6C 30
Laurel Cl. RG23: Oak 1B 22
　　RG29: N War 6C 20
Laurels, The RG21: B'toke 3E 16
　　SP10: A'ver 5D 36
Lauriston Ct. RG21: B'toke 5E 16
Lavender Cl. SP10: A'ver 1D 38
　　　　　　　　　　(off Floral Way)
Lavender Rd. RG22: B'toke 3G 23
LAVERSTOKE 5J 31
Laverstoke La.
　　RG28: L'stoke 7H 31
Lavington Cotts.
　　RG24: Old Bas 1K 17
Lawrence Cl. RG24: B'toke 7E 8
　　SP10: A'ver 4E 36
Lawrencedale Ct.
　　RG21: B'toke 5B 16
Lay Field RG27: Hoo 7K 11
Lea Cl. RG21: B'toke 5B 16
Leaden Vere RG29: L Sut 6D 28
Lees Hill RG25: Up G 5G 27
Lees Mdw. RG27: Hoo 7C 12
Lee Vw. SP11: Up C 3D 38
Lefroy Av. RG21: B'toke 2E 16
Lehar Cl. RG22: B'toke 2K 23
Leicester Pl. SP10: A'ver 7F 37
Leigh Cl. SP10: A'ver 7H 37
Leigh Gdns. SP10: A'ver 7H 37
Leigh Rd. SP10: A'ver 7G 37
Leisure Park (Park & Ride) . . .4K 15
Lennon Way RG22: B'toke 2J 23
Lennox Mall RG22: B'toke 7A 16
Lennox Rd. RG22: B'toke 7A 16
Len Smart Ct. RG21: B'toke . . .1E 16
Lewis Cl. RG21: B'toke 2E 16
Leyton Way SP10: A'ver 1C 38
Lightfoot Gro. RG21: B'toke . . .7D 16
Lights, The
　　Andover 6F 37
Lightsfield RG23: Oak 7B 14
Lilac Cl. SP10: A'ver 7C 36
Lilac Way RG23: B'toke 3K 15
Lillymill Chine RG24: Old Bas . .6J 9

Lillywhite Cres. SP10: A'ver . . . .2?
Lily Cl. RG22: B'toke . . . . .2?
Limbrey Hill RG25: Up G . . . . . . .5?
Lime Gdns. RG21: B'toke . . . . . . .4?
Limes, The RG24: B'toke . . . . . . .2?
　　RG26: B'ley . . . . .2?
Lime Tree Way RG24: Chin . . . . .5?
Lime Wlk. SP10: A'ver . . . . .5?
Lincoln Cl. RG22: B'toke . . . . . . .3?
Linden Av. RG24: Old Bas . . . . . .4?
　　RG29: Odi . . . . .5?
Linden Ct. RG24: Old Bas . . . . . .4?
Lindenwood RG24: Chin . . . . . . .5?
Lindsay Cl. RG28: Whit . . . . .5?
Lingdale Cl. SP10: A'ver . . . . . . .6?
Lingen Cl. SP10: A'ver . . . . .6?
Lingfield Cl.
　　RG24: Old Bas . . . . .4?
Link, The SP10: A'ver . . . . .6?
Link Way RG23: Oak . . . . .6?
Linnet Cl. RG22: B'toke . . . . .7?
Linton Dr. SP10: A'ver . . . . .6?
Lion Cl. RG25: Over . . . . .4?
Lion Ct. RG24: B'toke . . . . .2?
Lisa Ct. RG21: B'toke . . . . .5?
Lister Rd. RG22: B'toke . . . . .7?
Litchfield Cl. SP10: Charl . . . . . . .4?
Lit. Ann Rd. SP11: Abb A . . . . . . .3?
Little Basing RG24: Old Bas . . . . .2?
Little Binfields
　　RG24: Old Bas . . . .?
Little Copse SP10: A'ver . . . . . . .1?
Lit. Copse Chase RG24: Chin . . . .6?
Lit. Dean La. RG25: Up G . . . . . . .6?
Little Fallow RG24: Lych . . . . . . .1?
Little Hartleys RG27: Hoo . . . . . .7?
Little Hoddington
　　RG25: Up G . . . . .5?
Lit. Hoddington Cl.
　　RG25: Up G . . . . .5?
Litton Gdns. RG23: Oak . . . . . . .1?
Livia Cl. SP10: A'ver . . . . .2?
Livingstone Rd. SP10: A'ver . . . . .5?
Locksbridge La. RG26: B'ley . . . . .?
Locksmead RG21: B'toke . . . . . . .4?
Lock Sq. SP10: A'ver . . . . .4?
Loddon Bus. Cen.
　　RG24: B'toke . . . . .2?
Loddon Centre, The
　　RG24: B'toke . . . . .1?
Loddon Ct. RG21: B'toke . . . . . . .4?
Loddon Dr. RG21: B'toke . . . . . . .4?
Loddon Ho. RG21: B'toke . . . . . . .3?
Loddon Mall RG21: B'toke . . . . . .4?
Loddon Vale Indoor
　　Bowling Club, The . . . . . . .4?
Lodge Cl. SP10: A'ver . . . . .6?
Loggon Rd. RG21: B'toke . . . . . . .7?
Lomond Cl. RG23: Oak . . . . .7?
Loddon Rd. RG21: B'toke . . . . . . .5?
　　RG24: Old Bas . . . . .5?
　　RG25: Over . . . . .3?
　　RG27: H Win . . . . ?
　　RG27: H Win, Hoo, Nat S
　　. ?
　　RG27: Nat S . . . . .2?
　　RG28: Free, L'stoke, Whit
　　. .6?
　　RG29: Odi . . . . .6?
　　　　　　　　　　(not continuo?
　　SP10: A'ver . . . . .7?
　　SP11: A'ver, And D . . . .?
London St. RG21: B'toke . . . . . . .5?
　　RG28: Whit . . . . .6?
　　SP10: A'ver . . . . .6?
Longacre Ri. RG24: Chin . . . . . . .6?
Long Barn Rd. SP11: E Ant . . . . . .?
Longbourn Pl. RG24: B'toke . . . .1?
Longbridge Cl. RG27: Sher L . . . .4?
Longbridge Rd. RG26: B'ley . . . . .4?
Long Copse Chase
　　RG24: Chin . . . . .6?
Longcroft Cl. RG21: B'toke . . . . .5?
Long Cross La.
　　RG24: Chin . . . . .4?
Longfield RG23: Oak . . . . .8?
Longfield Cl. RG25: Nth W . . . . .2?
Long La. RG24: Old Bas . . . . .6?
　　　　　　　　　　(not continuo?
　　RG29: Odi, Wel . . . . .1?
Longmoor Rd. RG21: B'toke . . .?

parish Ct. *SP10: A'ver* 7G **37**
  (off Walled Mdw.)
roden La. RG25: Tun 4K **25**
s Ct. RG28: Whit 6C **30**
  (not continuous)
stock Cl. RG24: Chin 4K **9**
  SP10: A'ver 7D **36**
stock Cl. *SP10: A'ver* 7G **37**
  (off Walled Mdw.)
stock Rd. SP11: G Cla ...7F **39**
G SUTTON 7D **28**
wood Copse La.
  RG22: B'toke 6F **23**
  RG23: B'toke 6F **23**
Denning Ct.
  RG28: Whit 6C **30**
  (off Newbury Rd.)
sfield Gdns.
  RG25: Over 3C **32**
groves Rd. RG24: Chin 5J **9**
e La. RG29: Odi 2D **28**
  SP10: A'ver 7G **37**
eridge Cl. RG21: B'toke ..7C **16**
  SP10: A'ver 2G **37**
e Gdns. RG24: B'toke 7D **8**
Brook St. RG21: B'toke ..4B **16**
Chestnut Dr.
RG21: B'toke 6B **16**
Evingar Rd.
RG28: Whit 6C **30**
lands Rd. RG22: B'toke ..6G **15**
ry Ct. SP10: A'ver 5E **36**
alty La. RG24: Old Bas ...3K **17**
eck Dr. SP10: A'ver 3E **36**
ow Cl. RG23: B'toke 4J **15**
ow Gdns. RG23: B'toke ..4K **15**
dy Cl. RG24: B'toke 7F **9**
e Cl. RG21: B'toke 4F **17**
e Ct. SP10: A'ver 4H **37**
n Cl. RG22: B'toke 2G **23**
ens Cl. RG24: Lych 7H **9**
HPIT 1H **17**
e Cl. RG23: Oak 1B **22**
E GREEN 1H **11**
rd Rd. RG21: B'toke 3D **16**
ington Cl. RG22: B'toke ..3H **23**
CH 3A **32**
ch, The RG25: Over 3A **32**
RG28: Whit 6D **30**
CH HILL 6D **30**
ch Hill RG28: Whit 6C **30**
ch Hill Pk. RG28: Whit ..5D **30**
e Cl. RG21: B'toke 4F **17**
dhurst Dr. RG22: B'toke ..4J **23**
wood Dr. SP10: A'ver ...6D **36**
wood Gdns. RG27: Hoo ..7A **12**
el Combe RG27: Hoo 7D **12**
on Rd. RG21: B'toke 4E **16**

M

bbs La. RG27: H Win 4J **13**
helmyll Cft. RG27: Hoo ...7D **12**
cadam Way SP10: A'ver ..5A **36**
Cartney Wlk.
  RG22: B'toke 3J **23**
Fauld Way RG28: Whit ...7D **30**
deira Cl. RG24: B'toke ...7F **9**
drid Rd. SP10: A'ver 5H **37**
gellan Cl. SP10: A'ver ...5K **37**
gistrates' Court
  Basingstoke 5E **16**
gnolia Cl. SP10: A'ver ...7D **36**
gnolia Cl. RG24: B'toke ..7C **8**
gnus Dr. RG22: B'toke ...3H **23**
gpie Cl. RG22: B'toke ...2F **23**
nler Cl. RG22: B'toke 2B **24**
identhorn La.
  RG25: Nth W 2D **34**
iling Way RG24: Chin 1A **16**
ize Cl. SP11: E Ant 2H **37**
estic Rd. RG22: B'toke ..4G **23**
orca Av. SP10: A'ver 5H **37**
dive Rd. RG24: B'toke ...7F **9**
ham Gdns. RG27: H Win ..5H **23**
l, The *SP10: A'ver* 7F **37**
  (off Borden Gates)
lard Cl. RG22: B'toke 4G **37**
  SP10: A'ver 4G **37**
lory Rd. RG24: B'toke 7E **8**

Malls Shopping Centre, The
  RG21: B'toke 4D **16**
Malmesbury Flds.
  RG22: B'toke 2K **23**
Malshanger La. RG23: Oak ..5A **14**
Malta Cl. RG24: B'toke ...7D **8**
Maltings, The RG26: B'ley ..5C **4**
Malvern Cl. RG21: B'toke ..6G **15**
Manley James Cl.
  RG29: Odi 6E **20**
Mann Cl. RG24: Whit 7D **30**
Manor Cl. RG22: B'toke ...4G **23**
Manor Copse SP10: K Enh ..1G **37**
Manor Cotts. RG28: Free ..5H **31**
Manor Ho. RG26: Lych 1H **17**
Manor La. RG24: Old Bas ..3K **17**
Manor Ri. SP11: An V 3D **38**
Manor Ri. Flats SP11: An V .3D **38**
Manor Rd. RG24: Sher J ...5A **8**
  SP10: A'ver 5E **36**
Mansell Cl. RG28: Whit ...5C **30**
Mansfield Rd. RG22: B'toke .7A **16**
Manydown Pk.
  RG23: W Law 4C **14**
Maple Cl. RG21: B'toke ...5H **15**
Maple Cres. RG21: B'toke ..2D **16**
MAPLEDURWELL 6D **18**
Maplehurst Chase
  RG24: B'toke 4H **23**
Mapletons, The RG29: Odi .6F **21**
Maple Wlk. SP10: A'ver ...1C **38**
Maplewood RG24: Chin 5G **9**
Marchant Rd. SP10: A'ver ..7D **36**
March Cl. SP10: A'ver 4A **36**
Margaret Rd. RG22: B'toke .5K **15**
Marguerite Cl. RG26: B'ley ..4C **4**
Marigold Cl. RG22: B'toke ..2G **23**
Market Chambers
  RG21: B'toke 5D **16**
  (off Church St.)
Market Pl. RG21: B'toke ...5D **16**
  RG28: Whit 6C **30**
Mark La. RG21: B'toke 5D **16**
  SP10: A'ver 4A **36**
  SP11: Pen C 5A **36**
Marlborough Gdns.
  RG23: Oak 7B **14**
Marlborough St. SP10: A'ver .6F **37**
Marlborough Trad. M.
  RG24: Chin 6F **9**
Marlowe Cl. RG24: B'toke ..1E **16**
Marl's La.
  RG24: B'toke, Sher J 3D **8**
Marshall Gdns.
  RG21: B'toke 2D **16**
Marshall Sq. *SP10: A'ver* ...4H **37**
  (off Cricketers Way)
Marshcourt RG24: Lych 1H **17**
Marston Wlk. RG24: B'toke ..7C **8**
Marsum Cl. SP10: A'ver ...2E **36**
Martin Cl. RG21: B'toke ...2E **16**
Martins Wood RG24: Chin ...5H **9**
Martin Way SP10: A'ver ...4G **37**
Mary La. RG25: Nth W 1C **34**
Mary Rose Ct. RG21: B'toke .5B **16**
Maslen M. RG22: B'toke ...3J **23**
Mathias Wlk. RG22: B'toke ..4K **23**
Matilda Dr. RG22: B'toke ...3H **23**
Matrix Ho. RG21: B'toke ...4E **16**
Matthews Way RG23: Oak ..1C **22**
Mattock Way RG24: Chin ...5G **9**
Mauritius Cl. RG24: B'toke ..7F **9**
Maw Cl. RG22: B'toke 2B **24**
Maybrook RG24: Chin 4H **9**
May Cl. RG24: Old Bas 3A **18**
Mayfair Ho. *RG21: B'toke* ..4D **16**
  (off Festival Pl.)
Mayfield Ridge
  RG22: B'toke 5H **23**
Mayflower Cl. RG24: Chin ..6G **9**
Maynard's Wood RG24: Chin .6G **9**
May Pl. RG21: B'toke 5D **16**
May St. RG21: B'toke 4B **16**
May Tree Rd. SP10: A'ver ..5C **36**
Mead, The RG24: Old Bas ..3K **17**
Mead Cl. SP10: A'ver 7E **36**
Mead Gdns. RG27: H Win ..1H **13**
Mead Hatchgate RG27: Hoo .6A **12**
Mead Hedges SP10: A'ver ..1D **38**
  (not continuous)

Meadow Dr. SP11: G Cla ...7F **39**
Meadowland RG24: Chin 5G **9**
Meadow La. RG27: H Win ...2J **13**
Meadow Mobile Home Park, The
  RG27: Sher L 6G **5**
Meadowridge RG22: B'toke .4J **23**
Meadow Rise RG25: Nth W ..2D **34**
Meadows, The RG27: Sher L .6G **5**
Meadowside RG25: Up G ...5G **27**
Meadowside Ct.
  RG24: B'toke 1K **15**
Meadow Vw. RG28: Whit ...6B **30**
Meadow Way RG24: A'ver ..6C **36**
Mead Rd. SP10: A'ver 7E **36**
Mead Vw. SP11: G Cla 6F **39**
Mecca Bingo
  Andover 7F **37**
Mede Cl. RG25: Over 4D **32**
Medina Cl. *SP10: A'ver* 4H **37**
  (off Itchen Ct.)
Medina Gdns. RG23: Oak ...1B **22**
Medway Av. RG23: Oak 7B **14**
Medway Ct. RG21: B'toke ..4F **17**
  SP10: A'ver 4H **37**
Meitner Cl. RG26: B'ley 3C **4**
Melford Gdns. RG22: Wort ..7G **15**
Meliot Ri. SP10: A'ver 2F **37**
Melrose Wlk. RG24: B'toke ..1B **16**
Memorial Bungs.
  RG28: L'stoke 6H **31**
Memorial Rd. RG27: Hoo ...1A **20**
Mendip Cl. RG22: B'toke ...6G **15**
Meon Rd. RG23: Oak 1B **22**
Meon Wlk. RG21: B'toke ...4E **16**
Mercer Cl. RG22: B'toke ...5J **15**
Mercia Av. SP10: Charl 3C **36**
Meridian Office Pk.
  RG27: Hoo 1B **20**
Merlin Mead RG22: B'toke ..4F **23**
Merriatt Cl. RG21: B'toke ...7D **16**
Merrileas Gdns.
  RG22: B'toke 2G **23**
Merrydown La. RG24: Chin ..6J **9**
Merryfield RG24: Chin 5G **9**
Merryweather Way
  RG24: B'toke 6D **8**
Mersey Ct. RG21: B'toke ...4H **37**
Merton Rd. RG21: B'toke ...3B **16**
Messner St. RG24: B'toke ...7E **8**
Mews, The RG26: B'ley 5E **4**
  SP10: A'ver 1G **39**
Micheldever Gdns.
  RG28: Whit 7D **30**
Micheldever Rd.
  RG28: Whit 7C **30**
  SP10: A'ver 7G **37**
  SP11: A'ver 7G **37**
Middle Mead RG27: Hoo ...7A **12**
Middleton Gdns.
  RG21: B'toke 2D **16**
Midlane Cl. RG21: B'toke ...7C **16**
Midmay Ct. RG29: Odi 6E **20**
Mildmay Ter. RG27: H Win ..2K **13**
Milestones,
  Hampshire's Living History Mus.
  ....4A **16**
Milkingpen La.
  RG24: Old Bas 3K **17**
Millard Cl. RG21: B'toke ...2B **16**
Millbrook Cl. RG27: Sher L ..3J **9**
Mill Cl. RG27: Sher L 6H **5**
Millennium Ct. RG21: B'toke .4B **16**
Mill Field Local Nature Reserve
  ....2J **17**
Mill La. RG27: Stra S 1E **4**
  RG27: H Wes, Roth 7K **5**
  RG27: Newn 2F **5**
  RG29: N War 4B **20**
Mill Rd. RG24: B'toke 1J **15**
Millstream Cl. SP10: A'ver ..1E **38**
Mill Vw. RG29: Grey 7K **19**
Millway Cl. SP10: A'ver ...7D **36**
Millway Rd. SP10: A'ver ...7D **36**
Milton Av. SP10: A'ver 5C **36**
Milton Cl. RG24: B'toke ...1E **16**
Mimosa Cl. SP10: A'ver ...1D **38**
Minchens La. RG26: B'ley ...4B **4**
Minden Cl. RG24: Chin 6G **9**
Minshull Ct. SP10: A'ver ...6E **36**

Mitchell Av. RG27: H Win ..3J **13**
Mitchell Cl. SP10: A'ver ...5A **36**
Mitchell Gdns. RG22: B'toke .3J **23**
Moat Cl. RG26: B'ley 3C **4**
Monachus La. RG27: H Win ..1K **13**
Monarch Cl. RG22: B'toke ..4G **23**
Moneyer Rd. SP10: A'ver ..3E **36**
Mongers Piece RG24: Chin ..4J **9**
Moniton Est. RG22: Wort ...5H **15**
MONK SHERBORNE 2H **7**
Monk Sherborne Ho.
  RG26: M She 3H **7**
Monk Sherborne Rd.
  RG24: Sher J 3H **7**
  RG26: Cha A, Rams 1D **6**
  RG26: M She 2H **7**
Montague Rd. RG21: B'toke .6D **16**
Montserrat Pl. RG24: B'toke .6E **8**
Montserrat Rd. RG24: B'toke .6E **8**
Monxton Pl. RG27: Sher L ..3J **9**
Monxton Rd. SP10: A'ver ..6A **36**
  SP11: A'ver 7A **36**
Monxton Rd. Rdbt.
  SP11: A'ver 6A **36**
Moore Cl. SP10: A'ver 5F **37**
Moorfoot Gdns.
  RG22: B'toke 6H **15**
Moorhams Av. RG22: B'toke .4G **23**
Moorings, The RG21: B'toke ..4F **17**
Moor Vw. RG24: Old Bas ...2K **17**
Moot Cl. SP10: A'ver 2G **37**
Morgaston Rd.
  RG26: B'ley, M She 2K **7**
Morley Rd. RG24: B'toke ...1C **24**
Mornington Cl. SP10: A'ver ..2F **39**
Morris Ri. RG24: Chin 6D **8**
Morris St. RG27: Hoo 1J **19**
Morse Rd. RG22: B'toke ...5A **16**
Mortimer Cl. RG27: H Win ..4H **13**
Mortimer La. RG7: Stra S ...1E **4**
  RG21: B'toke 5C **16**
Moscrop Ct. RG21: B'toke ..5C **16**
Moths Grace RG24: B'toke ..1K **15**
Moulshay La. RG27: Sher L ..3A **10**
Mountbatten Cl. SP10: A'ver .5J **37**
Mountbatten Ho.
  RG21: B'toke 3F **17**
Mt. Pleasant RG27: H Win ..1K **13**
  RG28: Free 5H **31**
Mourne Cl. RG22: B'toke ...5H **15**
Mozart Cl. RG22: B'toke ...2A **24**
Mulberry Cl. RG27: H Win ..4J **13**
Mulberry Mead RG28: Whit ..6C **30**
Mulberry Way RG24: Chin ...5H **9**
Mull Cl. RG23: Oak 7A **14**
Mullins Cl. RG21: B'toke ...1D **16**
Munnings Cl. RG21: B'toke ..6F **17**
Munnings Ct. SP10: A'ver ..5E **36**
Murray Cl. RG27: H Win ...2E **38**
MURRELL GREEN 5E **12**
Murrell Green Bus. Pk.
  RG27: Hoo 6E **12**
Murrell Grn. Rd.
  RG27: H Win 3E **12**
Museum of the Iron Age 6G **37**
Musgrave Cl. RG22: B'toke ..2K **23**
Musket Copse
  RG24: Old Bas 3J **17**
Mustard Way SP11: E Ant ...2H **37**
Mylen Bus. Cen.
  SP10: A'ver 6D **36**
Mylen Rd. SP10: A'ver 6D **36**
Myllers Lond RG27: Hoo ...7D **12**

N

Napier Wlk. SP10: A'ver ...5J **37**
Napoleon Dr. RG23: B'toke ..2J **15**
Nash Cl. RG21: B'toke 2E **16**
Nash Mdws. RG29: S War ...6K **27**
Nately Rd. RG27: Up N 6H **19**
  RG29: Grey 6H **19**
Neath Rd. RG21: B'toke ...4F **17**
Nelson Wlk. SP10: A'ver ...5J **37**
Nene Ct. SP10: A'ver 4H **37**
Nestor Cl. SP10: A'ver 5E **36**
Netherfield Pl.
  RG24: B'toke 1A **16**
Neuvic Way RG28: Whit ...7D **30**

Neville Cl. RG21: B'toke 7D 16
SP10: A'ver 1G 39
Neville Ct. RG24: B'toke 2G 17
New Bridge La.
RG21: B'toke 4F 17
Newbury La.
SP11: Charl, Pen M 2A 36
Newbury Rd. RG28: Whit 6C 30
SP10: A'ver, K Enh 2F 37
SP11: Enh A 2F 37
Newbury Rd. Junc.
RG24: B'toke 2K 15
Newbury St. RG28: Whit 6C 30
SP10: A'ver 6G 37
Newcomb Cl. SP10: A'ver 2E 38
NEWFOUND 5C 14
Newman Bassett Ho.
RG23: B'toke 3J 15
Newman Ct. RG22: B'toke 2K 23
New Market Sq.
RG21: B'toke 4D 16
NEWNHAM 7G 11
Newnham La.
RG24: Old Bas 1K 17
RG27: Newn 7D 10
Newnham Pk. RG27: Hoo 1K 19
Newnham Rd.
RG27: Hoo, Newn 1H 19
New North Dr. RG27: Sher L . .1C 10
New Rd. RG21: B'toke 4D 16
RG26: B'ley 1B 8
RG27: H Win 2J 13
RG27: Hoo 1A 20
RG29: N War 5C 20
New St. RG21: B'toke 5D 16
SP10: A'ver 4G 37
New St. Cl. SP10: A'ver 6G 37
Newton Pk. SP10: A'ver 5A 36
Newtown Cl. SP10: A'ver 7D 36
Nightingale Gdns.
RG24: B'toke 1J 15
RG27: Hoo 7A 12
Nightingale Ri. RG25: Over . . .4D 32
Nobs Crook RG27: Hoo 7C 12
Norden Cl. RG21: B'toke 3D 16
Norden Ho. RG21: B'toke 3E 16
Norman Ct. La. SP11: Up C . . .2E 38
Normanton Rd.
RG21: B'toke 2D 16
Norn Hill RG21: B'toke 3E 16
Norn Hill Cl. RG21: B'toke . . .3E 16
Norrie Ct. RG24: B'toke 1J 15
Northbrook Cres.
RG24: B'toke 1J 15
Northcroft Ct. RG29: S War . .7A 28
Northern Av. SP10: A'ver 5F 37
Northern Retail Pk.
SP10: A'ver 5F 37
Northfield Rd. RG27: Sher L . .6G 5
Northgate Way RG22: B'toke . .4G 23
North Row RG26: B'ley 3C 4
NORTH WALTHAM 2C 34
Nth. Waltham Rd.
RG23: Oak . . . . .3A 22 & 4A 22
NORTH WARNBOROUGH 5C 20
North Way SP10: A'ver 4J 37
Norton Ho. RG22: B'toke 6J 15
Norton Ride RG24: Lych 2H 17
Norwich Cl. RG22: B'toke 3H 23
Novello Cl. RG22: B'toke 3K 23
Nursery Cl. RG24: Chin 5J 9
RG27: Hoo 6A 12
Nursery Ter. RG29: N War 5C 20
Nutbane Cl. SP10: A'ver 7C 36
Nuthatch Cl. RG22: B'toke . . .4F 23
Nutley La. RG25: Dumm 2K 35

O

Oak Bank SP10: A'ver 1F 39
Oak Cl. RG21: B'toke 4F 17
RG23: Oak 1B 22
RG25: Over 4C 32
Oakfields SP10: A'ver 1H 17
Oak Hanger Cl. RG27: Hoo . . .7B 12
Oakland Rd. RG28: Whit 6C 30
Oaklands RG27: H Win 3J 13
Oaklands Pk. RG27: Hoo 2J 19
Oaklands Way RG23: B'toke . . .3J 15

Oakland Ter. RG27: H Win 2K 13
Oaklea Gdns. RG26: B'ley 5E 4
OAKLEY 7A 14
Oakley La. RG23: Oak 1A 22
Oakley Pl. RG27: H Win 2K 13
(off High St.)
Oakmead RG26: B'ley 3B 4
OAKRIDGE 2D 16
Oakridge Ho. RG21: B'toke . . .2E 16
Oakridge Rd. RG21: B'toke . . .2B 16
Oakridge Towers
RG21: B'toke 2E 16
Oaks, The SP10: A'ver 6D 36
(off Lynwood Dr.)
Oaktree Dr. RG27: Hoo 6B 12
Oakwood RG24: Chin 5H 9
(Alderwood)
RG24: Chin 5G 9
(Maplewood)
Oakwood Ct. RG27: H Win 2J 13
Oasts, The RG29: L Sut 6D 28
Oat Rd. SP11: E Ant 2H 37
Oban Cl. RG23: Oak 7A 14
Oceana Cres. RG21: B'toke . . .6F 23
Ochil Cl. RG22: B'toke 6H 15
Octavian Cl. RG22: B'toke 3H 23
Odeon Cinema
Andover 7F 37
Basingstoke 4K 15
ODIHAM 6D 20
Odiham Castle (Remains of)
. . . . .5A 20
Odiham Rd. RG27: Winchf 4H 13
RG29: Odi 3F 21
Officers Row RG26: B'ley 5E 4
Olaf Cl. SP10: A'ver 2G 37
Old Barn Cl. RG25: Nth W 2C 34
OLD BASING 2K 17
Old Basing Mall
RG21: B'toke 4D 16
Old Beggarwood La.
RG22: B'toke 5G 23
Oldberg Gdns. RG22: B'toke . .2B 24
Old Brick Kiln Trad. Estate, The
RG26: Rams 1E 6
Old Canal Pl. RG21: B'toke . . .4F 17
Old Chapel La. RG26: Cha A . . .1F 7
Old Common Rd.
RG21: B'toke 5F 17
Old Down Cl. RG22: B'toke . . .2G 23
Old Down M. SP10: A'ver 5E 36
Old Down Rd. SP10: A'ver 5E 36
Oldenburg Cl. RG22: B'toke . . .3E 36
Old English Dr. SP10: A'ver . . .2E 36
Old Farm Dr. RG22: B'toke . . .6G 15
Oldfield Vw. RG27: H Win 3J 13
Old Kempshott La.
RG22: Wort 7G 15
Old Oak Cl. SP11: E Ant 2H 37
Old Orchard, The
RG29: S War 6K 27
Old Potbridge Rd.
RG27: Winchf 7G 13
Old Reading Rd.
RG21: B'toke 3E 16
Old Rectory, The
RG29: S War 6A 28
Old Salisbury Rd.
SP11: Abb A 4A 38
Old School, The
RG28: Whit 6C 30
(off Fairclose)
Old School Cl. RG27: H Win . . .2K 13
Old School Rd. RG27: Hoo 1J 19
Old Stable Yard, The
RG21: B'toke 5D 16
Old Winton Rd.
SP10: A'ver 7G 37
Old Worting Rd.
RG22: B'toke, Wort 5J 15
Olivers Cl. RG26: B'ley 5D 4
Oliver's La. RG26: B'ley 3D 4
Oliver's Wlk. RG24: Lych 2H 17
Onslow Cl. RG24: B'toke 7G 9
Optrex Bus. Pk.
RG27: Roth 4H 11
Orchard, The RG25: Over 4C 32
RG27: Hoo 6A 12
Orchard Lea RG27: Sher L 7G 5
Orchard Pl. RG28: Whit 6C 30
(off Church St.)

Orchard Rd. RG22: B'toke 5J 15
SP10: A'ver 5D 36
Orchid Ct. SP10: A'ver 1C 38
(off Floral Way)
Orkney Cl. RG24: B'toke 7F 9
Osborne Cl. RG21: B'toke 2C 16
Osborne Ct. SP10: A'ver 7F 37
(off Osborne Rd.)
Osborne Rd. SP10: A'ver 7E 36
Osborn Ind. Est. RG27: Hoo . .1B 20
Osborn Way RG27: Hoo 1B 20
Osler Cl. RG26: B'ley 4C 4
Osprey Rd. RG22: B'toke 1F 23
Otterbourne Wlk.
RG27: Sher L 3K 9
Ouse Ct. SP10: A'ver 4H 37
(off Nene Ct.)
Oval, The SP10: A'ver 3H 37
OVERTON 3D 32
Overton Hill RG25: Over 3D 32
Overton Ho. RG25: Over 3D 32
Overton Station (Rail) 1D 32
Owen Way RG24: B'toke 1K 15
Ox Drove
SP11: And D, Pic P 6K 37
Oxford Way RG24: B'toke 7C 8
Oyster Cl. RG22: B'toke 3H 23

P

Packenham Rd.
RG21: B'toke 6B 16
Pack La. RG22: B'toke 7G 15
RG23: Oak, Wort 6B 14
Paddington Ho.
RG21: B'toke 4D 16
(off Festival Pl.)
Paddock, The RG27: H Win . . .1K 13
Paddock Ct. RG27: H Win 3J 13
Paddock Flds.
RG24: Old Bas 2K 17
Paddock Rd. RG22: B'toke 6K 15
Paddock Wlk. RG22: B'toke . . .6K 15
Padwick Cl. RG21: B'toke 5C 16
Pages Bungs. RG21: B'toke . . .4E 16
Painters Pightle RG27: Hoo . . .7K 11
Palace Ga. RG29: Odi 6D 20
Palace Ga. Farm RG29: Odi . . .6D 20
Palmer Dr. SP10: A'ver 6J 37
Palmerston Pl. SP10: A'ver . . .6J 37
Pantile Dr. RG27: Hoo 7C 12
Papermakers RG25: Over 4D 32
Parade, The RG21: B'toke 3E 16
Parcel Dr. RG24: B'toke 2K 15
PARDOWN 3B 22
Pardown RG23: Oak 3B 22
Park & Ride
Leisure Park 4K 15
Park Av. RG24: Old Bas 4K 17
Park Cl. RG23: Oak 7A 14
Park Corner Rd.
RG27: H Win 1K 13
Park Gdns. RG21: B'toke 6E 16
Park Hill RG24: Old Bas 3J 17
PARKLANDS HOSPITAL 7K 7
Park La. RG24: Old Bas 4K 17
Park Prewett Rd.
RG24: B'toke 1J 15
Parkside Rd. RG21: B'toke 6E 16
Park Vw. RG28: Whit 7B 30
Parkview Ct. SP10: A'ver 4D 36
Parkwood Cl. RG24: Chin 4H 9
Parnell Ct. SP10: A'ver 5B 36
Partridge Cl. RG22: B'toke 3F 23
Pasture Wlk. SP11: E Ant 2H 37
Paterson Cl. RG22: B'toke 3J 23
Paulet Pl. RG24: Old Bas 3K 17
Paxton Cl. RG22: B'toke 3H 23
Paynes Mdw. RG24: Lych 1J 17
Peake Cl. RG24: Lych 2H 17
Pearman Dr. SP10: A'ver 6J 37
Pear Tree Way RG21: B'toke . . .2E 16
Pecche Pl. RG24: Old Bas 6J 9
Peel Ct. RG27: H Win 2J 13
Pegasus Cl. RG28: Whit 5C 30
Peggs Way RG21: B'toke 1K 15
Peked Mede RG27: Hoo 7D 12
Pekelond RG27: Hoo 7D 12
Pelham Cl. RG24: Old Bas 4K 17
Pelican Ct. SP10: A'ver 5G 37

Pelton Rd. RG21: B'toke 3I
Pemberley Pl. RG24: B'toke . . .1A
(off Priestley)
Pembroke Ct. SP10: A'ver 6I
Pembroke Rd. RG23: B'toke . . .4I
Pemerton Rd. RG21: B'toke . . .2I
Pen Cl. SP10: A'ver 7I
Pendennis Cl. RG23: B'toke . . .3I
Pendennis Ct. RG23: B'toke . . .3I
Pennine Cl. RG22: B'toke 6I
Pennine Way RG22: B'toke . . . .6.
Penny Black La.
RG24: B'toke 1A
Penrith Rd. RG21: B'toke 5I
Pensdell Farm Cotts.
RG25: Clid 1I
Pentland Cl. RG22: B'toke 6I
Pentney Cl. RG25: Over 4I
Penton Way
RG24: B'toke, Sher J 6
Percival Pl. RG24: Old Bas 4I
Pershore Rd. RG24: B'toke 7
(not continu
Pesthouse La. RG28: Whit 5I
Petersfield RG23: Oak 2I
Petersfield Cl. RG24: Chin 4
Petrel Ct. RG22: B'toke 2I
Petty's Brook Rd.
RG24: Chin 4
Petunia Cl. RG22: B'toke I
Petworth Cl. RG22: B'toke 4I
Peveral Wlk. RG22: B'toke 5I
Peveral Way RG22: B'toke 4I
Pewsey Cl. RG22: Wort 6G
Pexalls Cl. RG27: Hoo 7I
Pheaben's Fld. RG26: B'ley 4
Pheasant Cl. RG22: B'toke 2I
Pheby Rd. RG22: B'toke 7I
Phoenix Cl. RG27: H Win 4I
PHOENIX GREEN 4I
Phoenix Grn. RG27: H Win 4I
Phoenix Pk. Ter.
RG21: B'toke 3D
Phoenix Ter. RG27: H Win 4I
Picket Twenty SP11: A'ver 6I
(not continu
Picket Twenty Way
SP11: A'ver 7I
Picton Rd. SP10: A'ver 2I
Pigeonhouse La.
RG25: Far W 7A
Pigeons Cl. RG26: B'ley 5
Pilgrims Way SP10: A'ver 4I
Pillar Box Gdns.
RG24: B'toke 1A
Pimpernel Way
RG24: Lych 2I
Pines, The SP10: A'ver 6I
Pine Wlk. SP10: A'ver 1I
Pinewood Rd. RG24: Chin 5
Pinkerton Rd. RG22: B'toke . . .7.
Pinnell Cl. RG22: B'toke 4I
Pintail Cl. RG22: B'toke 3I
Pippin Sq. RG27: H Win . . . . . .4.
Pitcairn Cl. RG24: B'toke 6I
Pither Rd. RG29: Odi 3I
Pitman Cl. RG22: B'toke 7I
Pittard Rd. RG21: B'toke 4I
Pitts La. SP10: A'ver 1I
Planet Ice
Basingstoke . . . . .4.
Plantation, The
RG27: Sher L 7I
Plantation Rd. SP10: A'ver 7I
Plough Way SP11: E Ant 3I
Plover Cl. RG22: B'toke 1G
SP10: A'ver 4G
Poachers Fld. RG29: S War 4I
Poland La. RG29: Odi 3I
POLECAT CORNER 1K
POLHAMPTON 1I
Pond Cl. RG25: Over 5C
Pond Cotts. RG25: Clid 3I
Pond Rd. RG26: B'ley 5
Pool Rd. RG27: H Win . . . . . . .1.
Poors Farm Rd.
RG24: Old Bas 7I
POPHAM 7I
Popham La. RG25: Nth W 2I
Poplar Cl. RG27: Sher L 6I
POPLEY 3I

y Ponds Local Nature Reserve
..........6D 8
Way Way RG24: B'toke 1B 16
y Cl. SP10: A'ver 7B 36
y Fld. RG24: Lych 1J 17
ester Cl. SP10: Charl ...3C 36
ester Sq.
RG21: B'toke 4D 16
(off Festival Pl.)
cre Ri. RG21: B'toke 6B 16
l Cl. SP11: A'ver 7A 36
r Cl. RG29: Odi 2C 28
r Rd. RG22: B'toke 1B 24
rs Cl. RG25: Dumm 2H 35
SP10: A'ver 5C 36
and Gro. SP10: A'ver ..6F 37
mouth Cres.
RG22: B'toke 7K 15
mouth Wlk.
RG22: B'toke 7K 15
mouth Way
RG22: B'toke 7K 15
way Cl. SP10: A'ver 6C 36
way Ind. Est.
SP10: A'ver 5B 36
(Caxton Cl., not continuous)
SP10: A'ver 5A 36
(Telford Gate)
way Pl. RG23: B'toke ...4H 15
way Rdbt. SP10: A'ver ..4B 36
Corner RG21: B'toke ...1A 16
Horn La. RG27: Roth ...3J 11
Office La.
RG25: Dumm 2H 35
RIDGE 1G 21
ridge Rd. RG29: Odi ...2F 21
a. RG24: Old Bas 2D 18
rs La. RG27: Stra T 4J 5
rs Wlk. RG21: B'toke ...4D 16
(off Festival Pl.)
tons Cl. RG25: Over 4C 32
tons Rd. RG25: Over ...4C 32
d Cl. RG26: B'ley 4B 4
d Mdw. RG27: Sher L ..7H 5
RG28: Whit 6D 30
d Rd. RG25: Over 4D 32
erleague
Basingstoke 1K 23
lingbroke RG27: Hoo ...7D 12
ings Ens
RG21: B'toke 7E 16
ters Cl. SP10: A'ver 4E 36
tz Rd. RG25: Over 3C 32
celly Cl. RG22: B'toke ..5H 15
st Down RG21: B'toke ..5H 23
stley Rd. RG24: B'toke ..1A 16
rose Ct. SP10: A'ver 1C 38
(off Floral Way)
rose Dr. RG27: H Win ...1K 13
rose Gdns.
RG22: B'toke 5H 23
ce Albert Gdns.
SP10: A'ver 7F 37
(off The Elms)
ce Cl. SP10: A'ver 4J 37
ces Cres. RG22: B'toke ..6A 16
s Row RG19: A'ver 5C 20
y Gdns. RG24: Old Bas ..2K 17
y La. RG27: H Win 4H 13
RG28: Free 3G 31
ma Pk. RG24: B'toke ...1G 17
ett Cl. RG24: Lych 1J 17
pect Vs. RG22: B'toke ..7B 16
n Cl. RG22: B'toke 4F 23
house Way
RG21: B'toke 1K 15
ell Cl. RG22: B'toke 1B 24
enham Rd. RG24: Chin ..5J 9
ts Copse RG24: Old Bas ..7J 9
ts Ct. RG24: Old Bas ...7J 9
T'S HILL 7J 9
t's Hill RG24: Old Bas ..6J 9

Q

Sports Cen. 6D 16
ntock Cl. RG22: B'toke ..6H 15
en Anne's Wlk.
RG21: B'toke 4D 16
(off Festival Pl.)

Queen Mary Av.
RG21: B'toke 3D 16
Queens Av. SP10: A'ver ...6F 37
Queensdale Ct.
RG21: B'toke 6C 16
(off Pittard Rd.)
Queensfield RG25: Dumm ...2H 35
Queens Mead Gdns.
RG29: Odi 6D 20
Queen's Pde. RG21: B'toke ..4D 16
Queens Rd. RG21: B'toke ..4B 16
RG28: Whit 7D 30
RG29: N War 6C 20
Queensway SP10: A'ver ...4J 37
QUIDHAMPTON 2D 32
Quilter Rd. RG22: B'toke ..1J 23
Quince Tree Way RG27: Hoo ..7B 12

R

Rack Cl. SP10: A'ver 6G 37
Radford Gdns. RG21: B'toke ..7B 16
Raglan Cl. RG22: B'toke ..2J 23
Railway Cotts. RG23: Wort ..5F 15
RG24: Old Bas 3H 17
Rainbow Cl. RG24: Old Bas ..4A 18
Rainham Cl. RG22: B'toke ..3F 23
Rake Way SP11: E Ant 3H 37
Ramparts, The SP10: A'ver ..1D 38
Rampton Rd. RG28: Whit ..7D 30
RAMSDELL 1D 6
Ramsdell Rd.
RG26: Cha A, M She 1F 7
Ramsholt Cl. RG25: Nth W ..1C 34
Rankine Rd. RG24: B'toke ..2F 17
Raphael Cl. RG21: B'toke ..6F 17
Ravel Cl. RG22: B'toke 1A 24
Raven Rd. RG27: Hoo 7A 12
Ravenscroft RG27: Hoo 6B 12
Rawdon Cl. RG24: Old Bas ..4B 18
Rawlings Rd. RG27: Hoo ...1B 20
Rayleigh Rd. RG21: B'toke ..5D 16
Reading Rd.
RG24: B'toke, Chin 1F 17
(not continuous)
RG27: Hoo, Matt, Roth ...3B 12
RG27: Sher L 6H 5
Reading Rd. Rdbt.
RG21: B'toke 2F 17
SP10: A'ver 6G 37
Recreation Rd. RG29: Odi ..7D 20
SP10: A'ver 6G 37
Rectory Rd. RG23: Oak ...1A 22
RG27: Hoo 1A 20
Reculver Way SP10: A'ver ..3C 36
Redbridge Dr. SP10: A'ver ..7E 36
Redbridge La.
RG24: Old Bas 4G 17
Redes Cl. RG24: B'toke ...7D 12
Red Lion La. RG21: B'toke ..5D 16
RG25: Over 3C 32
Red Lion M. RG29: Odi ...6E 20
Redon Way SP10: A'ver 5E 36
RED RICE 6A 38
Red Rice Rd.
SP11: Red R, Up C 6A 38
Redwing Rd. RG24: B'toke ..3F 23
Redwood RG24: Chin 5G 9
Regal Hgts. RG29: Odi 6D 20
Regent Ct. RG21: B'toke ..3E 16
Regents Ct. SP10: A'ver ...5K 3
Reith Way SP10: A'ver 5A 36
Rembrandt Cl.
RG21: B'toke 6F 17
Remembrance Gdns.
RG24: Chin 6G 9
Rennie Ga. SP10: A'ver ...5B 36
Renoir Cl. RG21: B'toke ...6F 17
Renown Way RG24: Chin ..4H 9
Restormel Cl. RG23: B'toke ..3H 15
Reynolds Cl. RG21: B'toke ..5G 17
Reynolds Ct. SP10: A'ver ..4E 36
Reynolds Ho. RG22: B'toke ..7J 15
(off Pinkerton Rd.)
Reyntiens Vw. RG29: Odi ..7E 20
Rhodes Sq. SP10: A'ver ...3H 37
Ribble Ct. SP10: A'ver 4H 37
(off Itchen Ct.)
Ribble Way RG21: B'toke ..4F 17
Richards Fld. RG24: Old Bas ..6J 9
Richardson Cl. RG26: B'ley ..5C 4

Richborough Dr.
SP10: Charl 3B 36
Richmond Rd.
RG21: B'toke 3C 16
Rickett La. RG27: H Wes ...1H 11
Ridge Cl. RG22: B'toke ...5J 23
Ridge La.
RG27: Newn, Roth 7H 11
Ridleys Piece RG29: S War ..6A 28
Riley La. RG24: Old Bas ...2K 17
Ringshall Gdns. RG26: B'ley ..4B 4
Ringway Centre, The
RG21: B'toke 2B 16
Ringway East RG21: B'toke ..2F 17
Ringway Ho. RG24: B'toke ..2F 17
Ringway Nth. RG21: B'toke ..2A 16
RG24: B'toke 2J 15
Ringway Sth. RG21: B'toke ..7C 16
Ringway West RG21: B'toke ..2A 16
Ripley Ter. RG27: Sher L ...3K 9
Risinghurst M. RG24: B'toke ..7C 8
Riverside SP11: G Cla 5F 39
Riverside Cl. RG24: Old Bas ..1K 17
RG25: Over 3D 32
River Way SP10: A'ver 4G 37
Robert Mays Rd. RG29: Odi ..7C 20
Robin Cl. RG22: B'toke ...2G 23
Robin Way SP10: A'ver 4G 37
Rochester Cl. RG22: B'toke ..2H 23
Rochford Rd. RG21: B'toke ..4C 16
Rockbourne Rd.
RG27: Sher L 3J 9
Roding Cl. RG21: B'toke ...4F 17
Rodney Cl. SP10: A'ver 5J 37
Roentgen Rd. RG24: B'toke ..2G 17
Roke La. RG29: Odi 1G 29
Roman Ho. RG23: B'toke ..4H 15
Roman Rd.
RG23: B'toke, Wort 5G 15
Roman Way RG23: Wort ...5G 15
SP10: A'ver 2G 37
Romney Rd. SP11: E Ant ..2H 37
Romsey Cl. RG24: B'toke ..7C 8
Romsey Rd.
SP11: G Cla, Wher 6H 39
Rookery, The RG28: Whit ..6C 30
Rooksbury Mill Ct.
SP10: A'ver 1D 38
Rooksbury Rd. SP10: A'ver ..1D 38
Rooksdown Av. RG24: B'toke ..1J 15
Rooksdown La.
RG24: B'toke 1H 15
Rookswood Cl. RG27: Hoo ..7B 12
Rosebay Gdns. RG27: Hoo ..6C 12
Roseberry Cl. RG22: B'toke ..5H 23
Rose Cl. RG22: B'toke 2H 23
Rose Estate, The
RG27: Hoo 1B 20
Rosefield Cl. RG27: H Win ..1K 13
Rosehip Way RG24: Lych ..2H 17
Rose Hodson Pl.
RG23: B'toke 2J 15
Rosewood RG24: Chin 5G 9
Ross Cl. RG21: B'toke 7C 16
Rossetti Cl. RG24: B'toke ..1E 16
Rossini Cl. RG22: B'toke ..2A 24
Rothay Cl. RG21: B'toke ..4F 17
ROTHERWICK 3J 11
Rotherwick La.
RG27: H Wes, Roth 1F 11
Rotten Hill RG25: Over 5J 31
RG28: L'stoke 5J 31
Roundmead Ct.
RG21: B'toke 5C 16
Roundtown RG25: Tun ...2K 25
Roundway SP10: A'ver 6D 36
Row, The RG27: H Win ...2K 13
(off High St.)
Rowner Cres. RG27: Sher L ..3J 9
Royal Cl. RG22: B'toke ...5G 23
Royce Cl. SP10: A'ver 5A 36
Rubens Cl. RG21: B'toke ..7F 17
Rune Dr. SP10: A'ver 2E 36
Rushes, The RG21: B'toke ..4F 17
Ruskin Cl. RG21: B'toke ..6G 17
Russell Rd. RG21: B'toke ..6D 16
Rutherford Rd.
RG21: B'toke 1F 17
Rycroft Mdw. RG22: B'toke ..6G 23
Rydal Cl. RG22: B'toke ...7G 15
Ryeland Way SP11: E Ant ..2J 37

Rye Way SP11: E Ant 2H 37
Ryon Cl. SP10: A'ver 2F 37

S

Saffron Cl. RG24: Chin ...4J 9
Sainfoin La. RG23: Oak ...2B 22
Sainsbury Cl. SP10: A'ver ..1E 38
St Alphege Gdns.
SP10: A'ver 4E 36
St Andrew's Rd.
RG22: B'toke 6K 15
(not continuous)
St Annes Cl. SP11: G Cla ..6E 38
St Ann's Cl. SP10: A'ver ..7E 36
St Barbara's Cl. RG26: B'ley ..5E 4
St Birinus Gdns. SP10: A'ver ..3E 36
St Birstan Gdns. SP10: A'ver ..4E 36
St Christophers Cl.
RG22: B'toke 6J 15
St Davids Cl. RG29: Odi ..7C 20
St David's Rd. RG22: B'toke ..6A 16
St Gabriels Lea RG24: Chin ..5J 9
St Hubert Rd. SP10: A'ver ..7D 36
St James' Cl. RG26: B'ley ..5E 4
St John Cl. RG26: B'ley 5D 4
St John's Cl. RG27: Hoo ..7B 12
St John's Cotts. RG22: Hoo ..1J 19
St John's Piece RG23: Oak ..2B 22
St Johns Rd. RG23: Oak ...7B 14
RG27: H Win 3K 13
SP10: A'ver 6G 37
St Johns Wlk. RG21: B'toke ..4D 16
(off Festival Pl.)
St Joseph's Cres. RG24: Chin ..6H 9
St Leonards Av. RG24: Chin ..5J 9
St Lukes Cl. RG22: B'toke ..6J 15
St Marks Cl. RG26: B'ley ...5D 4
St Mary's Av. RG22: B'toke ..5E 4
St Mary's Cl. RG24: Old Bas ..3K 17
St Mary's Ct. RG21: B'toke ..4E 16
RG26: B'ley 5E 4
St Mary's Mdw.
SP11: Abb A 3A 38
St Mary's Rd. RG27: H Win ..3J 13
St Michael's Cl.
RG25: Nth W 2B 34
ST MICHAEL'S HOSPICE 7A 8
St Michael's Rd.
RG22: B'toke 6J 15
St Nicholas Ct. RG22: B'toke ..5K 15
St Patrick's Rd.
RG22: B'toke 6A 16
St Paul's Rd. RG22: B'toke ..6A 16
St Peter's Cl. SP11: G Cla ..5G 39
St Peter's Rd. RG22: B'toke ..6A 16
St Stephen's Cl. RG27: Up N ..4F 19
St Swithin Way SP10: A'ver ..4E 36
St Thomas Cl. RG21: B'toke ..2C 16
SP10: Charl 3D 36
Salisbury Cl. RG29: Odi ..7C 20
Salisbury Gdns.
RG22: B'toke 5J 15
Salisbury Rd. SP10: A'ver ..1C 38
SP11: Abb A, An V 5A 38
Salmond Rd. SP11: A'ver ..6A 36
Salmons Rd. RG29: Odi ..7C 20
SALTERS HEATH 1K 7
Salters Heath Rd.
RG26: M She 6H 7
Sam Whites Hill SP11: Up C ..3D 38
Sandbanks Dr. RG27: B'toke ..3H 23
Sand Martin Cl. RG26: Cha A ..1F 7
Sandpiper Way RG22: B'toke ..3F 23
Sandringham Ct.
RG22: B'toke 6K 15
Sandringham Ho.
SP10: A'ver 3F 37
Sandy La. RG27: H Win ...3K 13
Sandys Cl. RG22: B'toke ..6A 16
Sandys Rd. RG22: B'toke ..5A 16
Sandys Rd. Rdbt.
RG22: B'toke 5A 16
Saor Rd. SP10: A'ver 6E 36
Sapley La. RG25: Over 4C 32
Sark Way RG24: B'toke ...7F 9
Sarum Hill RG21: B'toke ..5C 16
Sarum Rd. SP10: A'ver ...7F 37
Savoy Cl. SP10: A'ver 7G 37
Saxon Ct. SP10: A'ver 3F 37

Saxon Way RG24: Lych 2H 17
  SP10: A'ver 3E 36
Scarlatti Rd. RG22: B'toke 2B 24
Sceptre Ct. SP10: A'ver 5K 37
School Cl. RG22: Wort 5G 15
Schroeder Cl. RG21: B'toke 7C 16
Schubert Rd. RG22: B'toke 2A 24
Scotney Rd. RG21: B'toke 2D 16
Scots Ct. RG27: Hoo 6C 12
Scott Cl. SP10: A'ver 5K 37
Scott Ho. RG21: B'toke 3E 16
Scotts Cnr. RG22: B'toke 1B 24
  (off Harrow Way)
Scures Hill RG24: Nat S 2G 19
Scures Rd. RG27: Hoo 7K 11
Scythe Cl. SP11: E Ant 2H 37
Seagull Cl. RG22: B'toke 2F 23
Seal Rd. RG21: B'toke 4D 16
Searl's La. RG27: Hoo, Roth . . .4B 12
Sedge Rd. SP11: E Ant 2J 37
Seeviours Rd. RG28: Whit 6C 30
Selborne Cl. RG27: Hoo 7B 12
Selby Wlk. RG24: Winchf 7D 8
Seton Dr. RG27: Hoo 1K 19
Seventon Rd. RG25: Nth W 2C 34
Severals, The RG24: Sher J 5A 8
Severn Cl. SP10: A'ver 4H 37
  (off Itchen Ct.)
Severn Gdns. RG23: Oak 1B 22
Severn Way RG21: B'toke 4F 17
Seville Cres. SP10: A'ver 5H 37
  (not continuous)
Seymour Ct. RG29: Odi 6E 20
  (off Seymour Pl.)
Seymour Pl. RG29: Odi 6E 20
Seymour Rd. RG22: B'toke 7J 15
Shackleton Sq. SP10: A'ver 3H 37
  (off Cricketers Way)
Shakespeare Av.
  SP10: A'ver 5C 36
Shakespeare Rd.
  RG24: B'toke 1E 16
Shannon Ct. SP10: A'ver 4H 37
Shapley Heath
  RG27: Winchf 6H 13
Shaw Cl. SP10: A'ver 6B 36
Shaw Pightle RG27: Hoo 7K 11
Shears Ct. RG22: B'toke 2G 23
Shears La. SP11: E Ant 2H 37
Sheep Fair SP10: A'ver 6H 37
Sheep Fair Cl. SP10: A'ver 6H 37
Sheepwash Ct. RG24: B'toke . . .2K 15
Sheepwash La. RG26: Rams . . .2D 6
Sheldon's La. RG27: Hoo 7K 11
Sheldons Rd. RG27: Hoo 7A 12
Shelley Cl. RG24: B'toke 1E 16
Shepherds Row SP10: A'ver . . .7H 37
Shepherds Spring Cotts.
  SP10: A'ver 4F 37
Shepherds Spring La.
  SP10: A'ver 6F 37
Shepherds Wlk. RG23: Oak 7B 14
Sheppard Cl. RG28: Whit 7C 30
Sheppard Rd. RG21: B'toke 7C 16
Sheppard Sq. SP10: A'ver 4H 37
  (off Cricketers Way)
Sheraton Av. RG22: B'toke 3H 23
  RG24: Sher J 5A 8
SHERBORNE ST JOHN 5A 8
SHERFIELD GREEN 6G 5
SHERFIELD ON LODDON 7H 5
Sherfield Rd. RG26: B'ley 4C 4
  RG27: Sher L 5D 4
Sherrington Way
  RG22: B'toke 7B 16
Sherwood Cl. RG22: B'toke 4J 23
Shetland Rd. RG24: B'toke 7E 8
Shipton Way RG22: B'toke 7J 15
Shooters Way RG21: B'toke 3E 16
Shortwood Copse La.
  RG23: B'toke 5F 23
Shrivenham Wlk.
  RG24: B'toke 7D 8
Shrubbery Wlk.
  RG21: B'toke 7C 16
Sibelius Cl. RG22: B'toke 3A 24
Sidlaw Cl. RG22: B'toke 6G 15
Sidmouth Rd. SP10: A'ver 6H 37
Silchester Cl. SP10: A'ver 4D 36
Silchester Rd. RG26: B'ley 5A 4

Silk Mill La. RG25: Over 3B 32
Silkweavers Rd. SP10: A'ver . . .6G 37
Silver Birch Rd. SP10: A'ver . . .5D 36
Silvers Cl. RG26: Rams 1D 6
Silvester Cl. RG21: B'toke 2E 16
Simmons Wlk. RG21: B'toke . . .5E 16
Simons Cl. RG24: Chin 6H 9
Simons Rd. RG24: Chin 6G 9
Sims Cl. RG26: B'ley 5E 4
Sinclair Dr. RG21: B'toke 4B 16
Skippetts Gdns.
  RG21: B'toke 7D 16
Skippetts La. E.
  RG21: B'toke 7E 16
Skippetts La. W.
  RG21: B'toke 7D 16
Skylark Cl. RG22: B'toke 4F 23
Skylark Ri. RG28: Whit 5B 30
Slessor Cl. SP11: A'ver 7A 36
Smallfield Dr. RG27: Hoo 7C 12
Smannell Rd. SP10: A'ver 3G 37
  SP11: Sman 3G 37
Smannell Rd. Rdbt.
  SP10: A'ver 4F 37
Smeaton Rd. SP10: A'ver 4A 36
Smith's Fld. RG25: Over 4D 32
Smiths Mead RG25: Nth W 2D 34
Smith Wright Ter.
  RG22: B'toke 2C 24
Smithy, The RG26: B'ley 4C 4
Snowdrop Cl. RG22: B'toke 2G 23
Sobers Sq. SP10: A'ver 3H 37
Solby's Rd. RG21: B'toke 4C 16
Solent Dr. RG22: B'toke 5H 23
Somerville Ct. SP10: A'ver 5J 37
Sonning Cl. RG22: B'toke 3F 23
Soper Gro. RG21: B'toke 3D 16
Sopers Row RG24: Old Bas 3J 17
Sopwith Pk. SP10: A'ver 5A 36
Sorrell's Cl. RG24: Chin 5H 9
Sorting La. RG24: B'toke 1K 15
South Dr. RG27: Sher L 2B 10
South End Rd. SP10: A'ver 1G 39
Southend Rd. RG21: B'toke 4C 16
Southern Haye RG27: H Win . . .3J 13
Southern Rd. RG21: B'toke 5D 16
SOUTH HAM 6A 16
Sth. Ham Ho. RG22: B'toke 6J 15
South Ham Rd.
  RG22: B'toke 5A 16
South Hill RG25: Up G 5G 27
SOUTHINGTON 3B 32
Southington Cl. RG25: Over 4B 32
Southington La. RG25: Over 3B 32
Southlands RG24: Chin 5G 9
Southlea RG25: Clid 2C 24
South Ridge RG29: Odi 7E 20
South St. SP10: A'ver 1F 39
SOUTH VIEW 2D 16
South Vw. Cotts. RG27: Hoo . . .7A 12
South Vw. Gdns.
  SP10: A'ver 7G 37
Southview M. RG21: B'toke 2E 16
SOUTH WARNBOROUGH 7A 28
South Way RG21: B'toke 4J 37
SPANISH GREEN 5K 5
Speckled Wood Rd.
  RG24: B'toke 7D 8
Sperrin Cl. RG22: B'toke 6H 15
Spey Ct. SP10: A'ver 4H 37
Spindlewood RG24: Chin 4H 9
Spinney, The RG24: B'toke 1K 15
  (Peggs Way)
  RG24: B'toke 2A 16
  (Priestley Rd.)
  RG27: Hoo 6A 12
Spinney Ct. RG24: B'toke 1K 15
Spinney M. RG21: B'toke 1K 15
Spire Cl. RG24: B'toke 6D 8
  RG24: B'toke 1K 15
Spoonwood Cl.
  RG24: B'toke 1K 15
Sports Centre, The
  Basingstoke 4D 16
Sprats Hatch La.
  RG27: Dogm, Winchf 3K 21
Sprents La. RG25: Over 4D 32
Spring Cl. RG24: Sher J 5K 7
Springfield RG23: Oak 7C 14
Springfield Av.
  RG27: H Win 1J 13
Springfield Cl. SP10: A'ver 6J 37

Spring M. SP10: A'ver 5G 37
  (off Shepherds Spring La.)
Springpark Ho.
  RG21: B'toke 3E 16
Spruce Cl. SP10: A'ver 7B 36
Square, The RG21: B'toke 3E 16
  RG24: B'toke 1K 15
Squarefield Gdns.
  RG27: Hoo 6C 12
Squirrel Dr. RG23: B'toke 7F 23
Stable Cl. RG27: Hoo 7K 11
Stag Hill RG22: B'toke 7K 15
Stag Oak La. RG24: Chin 4G 9
Stanford Rd. RG22: B'toke 2J 23
Stanswood Grange
  RG27: Sher L 3J 9
Starling Cl. RG22: B'toke 2F 23
Statham Sq. SP10: A'ver 3H 37
Station App. RG21: B'toke 3D 16
  SP10: A'ver 6D 36
Station Downside
  RG27: Winchf 7K 13
Station Hill RG21: B'toke 3D 16
  RG25: Over 1D 32
  RG27: Winchf 6J 13
Station Mall RG21: B'toke 4D 16
Station Rd. RG23: Oak 7A 14
  RG25: Clid 3C 24
  RG25: Over 3D 32
  RG27: Hoo 7A 12
  RG27: Winchf 7K 13
  RG28: Whit 5C 30
Stephenson Rd. SP10: A'ver . . .5B 36
Stephenson Rd.
  RG21: B'toke 3A 16
Sterling Pk. SP10: A'ver 5B 36
STEVENTON 7K 33
Stewart Rd. RG24: B'toke 7G 9
Stiles Dr. SP10: A'ver 6J 37
Stockbridge Cl. RG24: Chin 4K 9
Stockbridge Rd.
  RG25: Nth W 4B 34
  SP11: Red R 7A 38
Stocker Cl. RG21: B'toke 7C 16
Stoken La. RG27: H Win 1F 13
Stokes La. RG24: Sher J 5H 7
  RG26: M She 5H 7
Stone Cl. SP10: A'ver 1D 38
Stonehills RG25: Stev 6K 33
Stonelea Gro. RG29: N War 3C 20
Stourhead Cl. SP10: A'ver 7D 36
Stour Rd. RG23: Oak 1B 22
Stratfield Rd. RG21: B'toke 2C 16
Stratfield Saye Rd.
  RG7: Stra S 2D 4
STRATFIELD TURGIS 3K 5
Strathfield Rd. SP10: A'ver 2E 38
Stratton Rd. RG21: B'toke 7B 16
Strauss Rd. RG22: B'toke 2J 23
Stravinsky Rd. RG22: B'toke . . .2B 24
Strawberry Flds. RG26: B'ley . . .3C 4
Street, The RG24: Old Bas 3J 17
  RG26: B'ley 5A 4
  RG27: Roth 3J 11
  RG29: Grey 7K 19
  RG29: L Sut 7D 28
  RG29: N War 6B 20
STREET END 2K 11
Street Mdw. RG29: S War 7A 28
Stroud Cl. RG24: Chin 6G 9
Stroud Grn. La. RG27: Roth 4G 11
Stroudley Rd. RG24: B'toke 1G 17
Stuart Ct. SP10: A'ver 3F 37
Stubbs Cl. SP10: A'ver 4E 36
Stubbs Rd. RG21: B'toke 7E 16
Stukeley Rd. RG21: B'toke 5B 16
Suffolk Rd. SP10: A'ver 7E 36
Sullivan Rd. RG22: B'toke 2K 23
Summerfields RG24: Chin 4J 9
Sunflower Cl. RG22: B'toke 3H 23
Sunflower Way SP11: E Ant . . .2H 37
Sunny Mead RG23: Oak 2B 22
Sunnyside Cl. SP10: Charl 4C 36
Sunwood Dr. RG27: Sher L 3J 9
Sutcliffe Sq. SP10: A'ver 3H 37
  (off Cricketers Way)
Sutherland Ct. SP10: A'ver 5F 37
  (off Artists Way)
Sutton Rd. RG21: B'toke 2D 16
Swallow Cl. RG22: B'toke 2F 23
Swallowfields SP10: A'ver 3G 37

Swan Ct. RG27: H Win . . . . . .
  SP10: A'ver . . . .
Swan M. RG29: N War . . . . . .
Swift Cl. SP10: A'ver . . . .
Swing Swang La.
  RG24: B'toke . . . .
  (not contir
Sycamore Wlk. SP10: A'ver . .
Sycamore Way RG23: B'toke . .
Sylvaner Ct. RG21: B'toke . . .
Sylvia Cl. RG21: B'toke . . . . .

T

Tallis Gdns. RG22: B'toke . . .
Talmey Cl. RG24: Chin . . . . .
Tamar Dr. RG23: Oak . . . . . .
Tamarisk Cl. RG22: B'toke . . .
Tangway RG24: Chin . . . . . .
Tanners Way RG23: Oak . . . .
Taplin Cl. RG24: B'toke . . . .
Taplin's Farm La.
  RG27: H Win, Winchf . . .
Tarrant Gdns. RG27: H Win . .
Taskers Dr. SP11: An V . . . .
Tasmania Cl. RG24: B'toke . .
Tate Sq. SP10: A'ver . . . . . .
Taverner Cl. RG21: B'toke . . .
Taylor Dr. RG26: B'ley . . . . .
Taylors La. RG27: Sher L . . .
Teal Cres. RG22: B'toke . . . .
Tedder Cl. SP11: A'ver . . . . .
Telford Gate SP10: A'ver . . .
Telford Ho. RG21: B'toke . . .
Telford Rd. RG21: B'toke . . .
Temple Towers RG21: B'toke .
Tempus Bus. Cen.
  RG21: B'toke . . . .
Tennyson Way RG22: B'toke .
Tenzing Gdns. RG24: B'toke .
Tern Cl. RG22: B'toke . . . . .
Terry Cl. RG22: B'toke . . . . .
Testbourne Ct. RG28: Whit . .
Test Ct. SP10: A'ver . . . . . .
Test M. RG28: Whit . . . .
Test Rd. RG28: Whit . . . . . .
Test Way RG21: B'toke . . . .
Tewkesbury Cl. RG24: B'toke .
Texel Grn. SP11: E Ant . . . .
Thackham's La.
  RG27: H Win . . . .
Thames Ct. RG21: B'toke . . .
  SP10: A'ver . . . .
The . . . .
  Names prefixed with 'The' fo
  example 'The Arboretum' are
  indexed under the main nam
  such as 'Arboretum, The'
Thistledown Cl. SP10: A'ver . .
Thorneycroft Ind. Est.
  RG21: B'toke . . . .
Thornhill Crossroads
  RG24: Chin . . . .
Thornhill Way RG24: Chin . . .
Thornton Cl. RG26: B'ley . . .
Thornycroft La.
  RG21: B'toke . . . .
Thornycroft Rdbt.
  RG21: B'toke . . . .
Thrush Cl. RG22: B'toke . . . .
Thumwood RG24: Chin . . . . .
Thurston Pl. RG21: B'toke . . .
Thyme Cl. RG24: Chin . . . . .
Tiberius Cl. RG23: B'toke . . .
Tiberius Rd. SP10: A'ver . . . .
Tigwells Fld. RG29: S War . .
Till Cl. SP11: E Ant . . . .
Timberlake Ct. RG21: B'toke .
Timberlake Rd.
  RG21: B'toke . . . .
  (Goat
  RG21: B'toke . . . .
  (Victory F
Timor Cl. RG24: B'toke . . . .
Tinley Gdns. RG29: Odi . . . .
Tintagel Cl. RG23: B'toke . . .
  SP10: A'ver . . . .
Tintern Cl. RG24: Chin . . . . .
Tippett Gdns. RG22: B'toke . .
Titchfield Cres. RG27: Sher L .

Mdw. RG22: B'toke 5J 23
ton Rd. RG23: B'toke 4H 15
ate Rd. RG24: B'toke 7D 8
do Gro. SP10: A'ver 5H 37
023: Oak 6B 14
ate Rd. SP10: A'ver 5C 36
ouse Cl. SP11: A'ver 7K 37
way RG24: Chin 4J 9
z Dr. SP10: A'ver 6C 36
ary, The RG24: Lych 1J 17
ga Wlk. RG24: B'toke 7F 9
ly Tennis
Basingstoke 5E 16
nham Cl. RG26: B'ley 3C 4
rs La. RG27: H Win, Odi ..5F 13
RG29: Odi 5F 13
ist Info. Cen.
Andover 6G 37
y Cl. SP10: A'ver 5J 37
er Cl. SP10: Charl 3C 36
argate Ind. Pk.
SP10: A'ver 7C 36
er Skyline Plaza, The
RG21: B'toke 4D 16
(off Alencon Link)
N CENTRE
RG21, Basingstoke 4D 16
n Centre East Junc.
RG24: Old Bas 4G 17
n Hall Ct. RG28: Whit ...6C 30
n Mill RG25: Over 3D 32
n Mill La. RG28: Whit ...6D 30
nsend Cl. RG21: B'toke ..5B 16
n Sta. Rdbt. SP10: A'ver .7F 37
n Wlk. SP10: A'ver 3G 37
oil Cl. RG27: H Win 1J 13
is Dr. RG24: Lych 1J 17
rchard Rd. SP11: A'ver ..6A 36
chmead Gdns.
RG24: B'toke 1J 15
t Ct. SP10: A'ver 4H 37
t Way RG21: B'toke 4F 17
as Cl. RG25: Over 3C 32
idad Cl. RG22: B'toke ...7D 8
rman Sq. SP10: A'ver ...3H 37
(off Cricketers Way)
o Pl. RG22: B'toke 2H 23
ot Rd. RG27: Hoo 7K 11
h's La. RG26: Cha A 1G 7
or Ct. SP10: A'ver 3F 37
p Cl. RG22: B'toke 3G 23
nel La. RG29: N War 5B 20
WORTH 5A 26
worth Rd.
RG25: Mapl, Tun 5C 18
GIS GREEN 4K 5
n Ct. SP10: A'ver 2G 37
(not continuous)
nberry Dr. RG22: B'toke ..5G 23
er Ct. RG21: B'toke 5G 17
ner Ct. SP10: A'ver 5E 36
bury Rd. RG23: Oak 7A 14
eedsmuir Cl.
RG22: B'toke 5H 15
nley La.
RG28: Col H, Free 1G 31
I Gate La. RG25: Over ...4D 32
I Gate Mdw. RG25: Over ..3D 32
nes Mdw. RG27: Hoo 7D 12
eld RG24: Sher J 5A 8
urst Pl. SP10: A'ver 1F 39
ney La.
RG27: Newn, Roth 7H 11
ney Pk. Golf Course 4H 11
e Cl. SP10: A'ver 4H 37
ells Cft. SP10: A'ver 6H 37
ne Cl. SP11: E Ant 2H 37

U

on St. SP10: A'ver 6G 37
(off East St.)
versity of Winchester
Chute House Campus ..4D 16
avon Cl. RG22: Wort 6G 15
Fallow RG24: Lych 2J 17
NATELY 5G 19
Chestnut Dr.
RG21: B'toke 6B 16
PER CLATFORD 3D 38

Upper Drove SP10: A'ver 6B 36
Up. Farm Rd. RG23: Oak 2B 22
Up. Sherborne Rd.
RG21: B'toke 2C 16
Up. Stroud Cl. RG24: Chin ..6G 9
UPPER WOOTON 6C 6
Upron Fld. Cl. RG22: B'toke .3H 23
Up Street RG25: Dumm 2F 35
RG25: Nth W 2C 34
Upton Cres. RG21: B'toke ...2C 16
UPTON GREY 4F 27
Upton Grey Rd. RG25: Up G .4F 27
RG29: Grey 2H 27

V

Vale, The RG23: Oak 1B 22
Valencia Way SP10: A'ver ...5G 37
Valley Mead SP11: An V 2B 38
Valley Ri. SP11: Up C 3D 38
Valmeade Cl. RG27: Hoo ...7B 12
Vanburgh Gdns.
RG22: B'toke 3H 23
Van Dyck Cl. RG21: B'toke .6G 17
Varndell Rd. RG27: Hoo 7K 11
Venice Cl. SP10: A'ver 3G 37
(not continuous)
Venture Rdbt. RG21: B'toke .6E 16
Verandah Cotts.
RG27: H Win 2K 13
(off High St.)
Verden Way SP10: A'ver 3E 36
Verdi Cl. RG22: B'toke 2K 23
Verity Sq. SP10: A'ver 3H 37
Vernhams M. RG22: B'toke .1K 15
Veronica Cl. RG22: B'toke ..3G 23
Vespasian Gdns.
RG24: B'toke 1J 15
Vespasian Rd. SP10: A'ver .3G 37
Vestry Cl. SP10: A'ver 6E 36
Vetch Fld. RG27: Hoo 7C 12
Viables Craft Cen. 1C 24
Viables Ind. Est.
RG21: B'toke 1C 24
Viables La. RG22: B'toke ...1D 24
Viables Rdbt. RG22: B'toke .1B 24
Vicarage Hill RG27: H Win ..3K 13
Vickers Bus. Cen.
RG24: B'toke 1A 16
Victoria Ct. SP10: A'ver 7E 36
Victoria Pl. RG22: B'toke ...5H 15
Victoria St. RG21: B'toke ...5D 16
Victory Rdbt. RG21: B'toke ..4C 16
Viewpoint RG21: B'toke 3F 17
Vigo Rd. SP10: A'ver 6G 37
Vigo Rd. Rdbt. SP10: A'ver .6G 37
Viking Way SP10: A'ver 2G 37
Village St. SP11: G Cla 5F 39
Vincent Dr. SP10: A'ver 6C 30
Vinery Cl. RG28: Whit 6C 30
Vinns La. RG25: Over 4B 32
Violet Cl. RG22: B'toke 3G 23
Viscount Ct. SP10: A'ver ...5K 37
Vitellius Gdns.
RG24: B'toke 1J 15
Vivaldi Ct. RG22: B'toke ...3A 24
Vivian Rd. RG21: B'toke ...2E 16
Vue Cinema
Basingstoke 4D 16
Vyne, The 2D 8
Vyne Mdw. RG24: Sher J ...4B 8
Vyne Rd. RG21: B'toke 3D 16
RG24: Sher J 4B 8
RG26: B'ley 6A 4

W

Wade Rd. RG24: B'toke 2G 17
Wagner Cl. RG22: B'toke ...2A 24
Wagon La. RG27: Hoo 6B 12
Walk, The RG27: Sher L 1C 10
Walled Gardens, The
RG29: S War 7A 28
Walled Mdw. SP10: A'ver ...6G 37
Wallin's Copse RG24: Chin ..6H 9
Wallis Cl. RG23: B'toke 3K 15
Wallis Dr. RG26: B'ley 5E 4
Wallis Rd. RG21: B'toke ...6D 16
Wallop Dr. RG22: B'toke ...4G 23

Walls Caravan Pk.
RG27: Hoo 6C 12
Walnut Tree Rd. SP10: A'ver .7E 36
Walnut Way RG21: B'toke ..2E 16
Walpole Gdns. RG27: H Win .1K 13
Walsh Rd. RG26: B'ley 5C 4
Waltham Ct. RG25: Over 3D 32
Waltham La.
RG25: Nth W, Over, Stev
.............5E 32 & 1A 34
Waltham Rd. RG25: Over ...3D 32
Walton Cl. RG22: B'toke ...1A 24
Walton Rd. RG21: B'toke ...3E 16
Walworth Ent. Cen.
SP10: A'ver 5J 37
Walworth Ind. Est.
SP10: A'ver 4K 37
Walworth Rd. SP10: A'ver ..4J 37
SP11: Pic P 4J 37
Walworth Rdbt. SP10: A'ver .5J 37
Warbleton Rd. RG24: Chin ..5J 9
Ward Cl. SP10: A'ver 4F 37
Warner Cl. RG24: B'toke ...6D 8
Warner Rd. SP10: A'ver 6E 36
Warnford Gro. RG27: Sher L .3J 9
Warren Cl. RG27: H Win 3K 13
Warren Way RG22: B'toke ..6J 15
Warwick Cl. RG28: Whit 6C 30
Warwick Rd. RG23: B'toke ..5H 15
Wash Brook RG27: Hoo 6A 12
Watch La. RG28: Free 5H 31
WATER END 2E 18
Water End La.
RG24: Old Bas 2D 18
Water End Pk. (Caravan Site)
RG24: Old Bas 2E 18
Wateridge Rd. RG21: B'toke .1E 16
Waterlily Cl. RG21: B'toke ..4F 17
Waterloo Av. RG23: B'toke ..2J 15
Waterloo Ct. RG28: Whit ...6C 30
SP10: A'ver 7F 37
Waterloo Ter. SP11: An V ...3C 38
Watermeadows, The
SP10: A'ver 2E 38
Watermills Cl. SP10: A'ver ..1E 38
Water Ridges RG23: Oak ...2B 22
Watertower Way
RG24: B'toke 1K 15
Water Way RG21: B'toke ...4F 17
Waterworks Cotts.
RG21: B'toke 4B 16
Watery La. SP10: A'ver 5G 37
SP11: Up C 3D 38
Watling End RG22: B'toke ..3H 23
Watlington RG27: Hoo 7D 12
Watson Acre SP10: A'ver ...6D 36
Watson Way RG23: B'toke ..2K 15
Watt Cl. SP10: A'ver 5B 36
Wavell Cl. RG22: B'toke 7A 16
Waverley Av. RG21: B'toke ..7C 16
Waverley Cl. RG29: Odi 6F 21
Wayside Rd. RG23: B'toke ..4H 15
Weale Cl. RG21: B'toke 3D 16
Weatherby Gdns.
RG27: H Win 2K 13
Weavers Cl. SP10: A'ver 6G 37
Weavers Piece RG27: Roth ..3J 11
Webb Cl. RG24: Chin 6H 9
Webbs Farm Cl. RG28: Whit .7C 30
Wedderburn Av.
RG22: B'toke 5H 23
Wedman's La. RG27: Roth ..2K 11
Wedman's Pl. RG27: Roth ..2K 11
Weir, The RG28: Whit 7C 30
Weir Rd. RG27: H Win 4H 13
Wella Path RG21: B'toke ...7B 16
RG22: B'toke 7B 16
Wella Rd. RG22: B'toke 7B 16
Well Cl. RG23: W Law 2E 14
RG25: Nth W 2C 34
Wellesley Ct. SP10: A'ver ..1F 39
Wellesley Rd. SP10: A'ver ..1F 39
Wellington Rd. SP10: A'ver .5E 36
Wellington Ter. RG23: B'toke .2J 15
Wells-in-the-Field La.
RG28: Whit 5F 31
Well's La. RG28: Whit 7B 30
Wellspring Ho.
RG22: B'toke 7J 15
(off Pinkerton Rd.)
Welton Ct. RG21: B'toke ...4C 16

Wentworth Cres.
RG22: B'toke 5G 23
Wesley Wlk. RG21: B'toke ..4D 16
(off Festival Pl.)
Wessex Av. RG29: Odi 1D 28
Wessex Cl. RG21: B'toke ...6C 16
Wessex Cres. RG29: Odi ...1D 28
Wessex Dr. RG29: Odi 1D 28
Wessex Gdns. SP10: A'ver ..6E 36
Wessex Grange RG27: Sher L .7H 5
Westbrook Cl. RG23: Oak ...2B 22
Westbrook Ct. RG22: Wort ..5G 15
Westbrooke Cl. SP10: A'ver .7F 37
Westdeane Ct. RG21: B'toke .5B 16
West End RG24: Sher J 4K 7
Western Av. SP10: A'ver 6F 37
Western Cross RG22: Wort ..7D 20
Western La. RG29: Odi 6D 20
Western Rd. SP10: A'ver 7F 37
Western Way RG22: B'toke ..7K 15
Westfield Ct. SP10: A'ver ...7G 37
Westfield Rd. RG21: B'toke ..6E 16
Westgate Cl. RG23: B'toke ..3H 15
WEST GREEN 3F 13
West Green House Gdns. ...3F 13
West Green Rd.
RG27: H Win 1F 13
WEST HAM 4K 15
West Ham Ct. RG22: B'toke .5J 15
West Ham Cl. RG22: B'toke .5J 15
West Ham Est. RG22: B'toke .5J 15
West Ham La. RG21: B'toke ..4A 16
RG22: Wort 5H 15
West Ham Rdbt.
RG22: B'toke 5K 15
Westlands Ho. RG21: B'toke .5C 16
West La. RG29: N War 4B 20
Westmarch Bus. Cen.
SP10: A'ver 4G 37
Westminster Cl.
RG22: B'toke 3H 23
Westminster Ho.
RG21: B'toke 4D 16
(off Festival Pl.)
Weston Cl. RG25: Up G 5F 27
WESTON CORBETT 7D 26
WESTON PATRICK 7E 26
Weston Rd. RG25: Up G 6E 26
W. Point Bus. Pk.
SP10: A'ver 5A 36
West Portway SP10: A'ver ...4A 36
Westray Cl. RG21: B'toke ...2F 17
Westside Cl. RG22: B'toke ..6K 15
West St. RG29: N War, Odi ..6B 20
SP10: A'ver 6F 37
(not continuous)
West Vw. SP10: A'ver 7F 37
West Way SP10: A'ver 5J 37
Wetherby Gdns. SP10: Charl .4D 36
Weybrook Ct. RG24: Sher J ..4K 7
Weybrook Pk. Golf Course ...7J 7
Weyhill Rd. RG27: Hoo 7C 12
SP11: A'ver, Pen C 5A 36
Weysprings Cl. RG21: B'toke .4F 17
Wharf, The RG29: Odi 5F 21
Wheatleys Cl. RG25: Stev ...7J 33
Wheeler Cl. RG28: Whit 7D 30
Wheelers Hill RG27: Hoo ...7C 12
Wheeler Way RG24: B'toke ..6C 8
Whinchat Cl. RG27: H Win ..1J 13
Whistler Cl. RG21: B'toke ...6F 17
WHITCHURCH 6C 30
Whitchurch Silk Mill 7C 30
Whitchurch Station (Rail) ..5C 30
Whitebeam Cl.
RG22: Wort 5G 15
White Hart La. RG21: B'toke .5E 16
RG26: Cha A 1E 6
Whitehead Cl. RG24: Lych ..2H 17
White Hill RG29: Wel 7G 29
White Ho. Cl. RG22: B'toke ..7K 15
White La. RG25: Up G 1F 27
RG25: W Cor 7C 26
White Oak Way SP11: An V ..3B 38
Whites Cl. RG27: Hoo 7K 11
Whitestones RG22: B'toke ..4J 23
Whitewater Ri. RG27: Hoo ..6C 12
Whitewater Rd.
RG29: N War 5C 20
Whitewood RG24: Chin 5H 9
Whitgift Cl. RG21: B'toke ...5H 23

Whitmarsh La. RG24: Chin 5K **9**
RG27: Sher L 5A **10**
Whitney Rd. RG24: B'toke ...2G **17**
Whittle Rd. SP10: A'ver 5A **36**
Whynot La. SP10: A'ver 6D **36**
Wickham Way RG27: Sher L ...3K **9**
Wicklow Cl. RG22: B'toke 6H **15**
Widmore Rd. RG22: B'toke ...7J **15**
Wights Wlk. RG22: B'toke ...3H **23**
Wild Herons RG27: Hoo 7C **12**
WILDMOOR 3D **10**
Wildmoor La. RG27: Sher L ...7H **5**
Willis Museum, The 5D **16**
Willoughby Way
RG23: B'toke 3K **15**
Willow Gro. SP10: A'ver 7E **36**
Willows, The RG23: Oak 2A **22**
RG29: N War 5C **20**
SP10: A'ver 1E **38**
Willow Way RG23: B'toke ...2K **15**
RG27: Sher L 6G **5**
Wilmott Way RG23: B'toke ...3K **15**
Wilton Pl. RG22: B'toke 5B **16**
Wiltshire Cres.
RG22: Wort 6G **15**
Wimborne Cl. RG22: B'toke ..5G **23**
Winchcombe Rd.
RG21: B'toke 5C **16**
Winchester Gdns.
SP10: A'ver 1G **39**
Winchester Rd.
RG21: B'toke 6B **16**
RG22: B'toke 6E **22**
(not continuous)
RG23: B'toke 6E **22**
RG28: Whit 7C **30**
SP10: A'ver 2F **39**
SP11: A'ver, G Cla, Wher
.....................2F **39**
Winchester Rd. Rdbt.
RG21: B'toke 6B **16**
Winchester St. RG21: B'toke ..5D **16**
RG25: Over 3D **32**
RG28: Whit 7C **30**
SP10: A'ver 7G **37**

WINCHFIELD 6J **13**
Winchfield Station (Rail) 6J **13**
Windermere Av.
RG22: B'toke 7G **15**
Windmill La. SP11: An V ...3B **38**
Windover St. *RG21: B'toke* ...5D **16**
(off New St.)
Windrush Cl. *RG21: B'toke* ...4F **17**
(off Severn Way)
Windsor Gdns.
RG22: B'toke 4G **23**
Windsor Rd. SP10: A'ver 6E **36**
Wingate La. RG29: L Sut ...7D **28**
WINKLEBURY 3J **15**
Winklebury Cen.
RG23: B'toke 4J **15**
Winklebury Way
RG23: B'toke 2K **15**
Winkworth Bus. Pk.
RG27: H Win 5G **13**
WINSLADE 5G **25**
Winslade La.
RG25: Elli, Winsl 7F **25**
Winston Ho. RG21: B'toke ...4B **16**
Winterbourne Ho.
RG22: B'toke 7J **15**
(off Pinkerton Rd.)
Winterdyne M. SP10: A'ver ...7E **36**
Winterthur Way
RG21: B'toke 4C **16**
Winton Chase
SP10: A'ver 6J **37**
Winton Sq. SP10: A'ver 5D **16**
Wisley Rd. SP10: A'ver 7C **36**
Wistaria Ct. SP10: A'ver 7C **36**
Witan Cl. SP10: A'ver 2G **37**
Witan Ct. RG28: Whit 5B **30**
Wither Ri. RG23: Oak 7A **14**
Woburn Gdns.
RG22: B'toke 6J **15**
Wolds, The RG22: B'toke ...6H **15**
Wolversdene Cl.
SP10: A'ver 7H **37**
Wolversdene Gdns.
SP10: A'ver 7H **37**

Wolversdene Rd.
SP10: A'ver 7G **37**
Woodbury Rd. RG22: B'toke ..3H **23**
Wood Cl. RG22: B'toke 4H **23**
Woodcroft RG23: Oak 2B **22**
Wood End RG24: Chin 6G **9**
Woodgarston Dr.
RG22: B'toke 4G **23**
Woodgarston La.
RG26: Up Woott 1C **14**
Wood Hill La.
RG29: L Sut, Odi 6D **28**
Woodland Ct.
RG23: B'toke 5F **23**
Woodland Dr. RG26: B'ley 5E **4**
Woodlands RG24: Chin 4J **9**
RG25: Over 3C **32**
Woodlands Bus. Village
RG21: B'toke 3F **17**
Woodlands Way
SP10: A'ver 6H **37**
Wood La. RG27: Up N 4G **19**
Woodmanfield RG25: Up G ...5G **27**
Woodmere Cft. RG22: B'toke ..3F **23**
Woodpecker Cl.
RG22: B'toke 2F **23**
Woodroffe Dr. RG22: B'toke ...1J **23**
Woodside Gdns. RG24: Chin ...4J **9**
Woods La. RG25: Clid 3A **24**
RG29: Grey 5K **19**
Woodstock Ct. RG21: B'toke ...4C **16**
Woodstock Mead
RG22: B'toke 4H **23**
Woodville Cl. RG24: Chin 5H **9**
Woodville La. RG24: Chin 6H **9**
Woodville Ri. RG24: Chin 6H **9**
Wood Wlk. RG26: Rams 3A **6**
Wooldridge Cres.
RG29: Odi 2C **28**
Woolford Way
RG23: B'toke 3K **15**
Wool Gro. SP10: A'ver 7H **37**
Woolley Sq. SP10: A'ver 3H **37**
Woolston Pl. RG27: Sher L ...3J **9**
Wootton Cl. RG23: W Law ...2F **15**

Wootton La. RG23: W Law ...5
RG26: Up Woott ....
WOOTTON ST LAWRENCE ...2
Worcester Av.
RG22: B'toke 3
Wordsworth Cl.
RG24: B'toke 1
Worrell Sq. SP10: A'ver
(off Cricketers
Worsam Ct. RG22: B'toke ...5
WORTING 5
Worting Rd. RG21: B'toke ...5
RG22: B'toke, Wort 5
RG23: Newf, Wort 6
Worting Rd. Rdbt.
RG22: B'toke 5
Wote St. RG21: B'toke 5
Wrekin Cl. RG22: B'toke 2
Wren Cl. RG22: B'toke 2
Wye Ct. SP10: A'ver 4
Wykeham Ct. RG29: Odi 2
Wykeham Dr. RG23: Wort ...5
Wylie Gdns. RG24: B'toke ...
Wyndham Rd. SP10: A'ver ...1

Y

Yellowhammer Rd.
RG22: B'toke 3
Yew Tree Cl. RG23: Oak 2
RG26: B'ley ....
SP11: G Cla 6
Yew Tree Rd.
RG25: Nth W 2
Yew Tree Wlk. SP10: A'ver ...7
York Cl. RG22: B'toke 2
York Ct. SP10: A'ver 3
York Ho. RG22: B'toke 6
York La. RG27: H Win 3

Z

Zinnia Cl. RG22: B'toke 4